Inspired Ikebana

Modern Design Meets the Ancient Art of Japanese Flower Arrangement

Naoko Zaima

yellow pear press

Coral Gables

Cover Design: Elina Diaz
Cover Photo/illustration: Naoko Zaima
Layout & Design: Elina Diaz

For permission requests, please contact the publisher at:
Mango Publishing Group
2850 S Douglas Road, 4th Floor
Coral Gables, FL 33134 USA
info@mango.bz

For special orders, quantity sales, course adoptions and corporate sales, please email the publisher at sales@mango.bz. For trade and wholesale sales, please contact Ingram Publisher Services at customer. service@ingramcontent.com or +1.800.509.4887.

Inspired Ikebana: Modern Design Meets the Ancient Art of Japanese Flower Arrangement

Library of Congress Cataloging-in-Publication number: 2022935520
ISBN: (print) 978-1-64250-862-8, (ebook) 978-1-64250-863-5
BISAC category code CRA010000, CRAFTS & HOBBIES / Flower Arranging

Printed in China

For my son Takuma,
who is the most lovely flower in my entire life.

Contents

Part One:

The History of Ikebana

Ikebana, the Japanese art of arranging flowers, has a long, rich history created over many centuries. There are various theories about the origin of Ikebana, so I have attempted to introduce it here to give a sense of all that goes into this complex, yet simple, art.

One theory is that Ikebana began as a Buddhist flower ritual, when Buddhism was introduced to Japan around the sixth century. Others believe it came from the ancient Japanese custom of decorating evergreen trees with flowers as a way to invoke the gods. In any case, it seems certain that the development of Ikebana expresses the unique spiritual and heartfelt connection Japanese people have toward flowers and plants.

Ikebana first appeared in literature and art in the Muromachi period (late fourteenth to mid-sixteenth century). During this time, various unique Japanese cultural practices were created. In addition to the tradition of Buddhist Ikebana, Tatebana (which refers to "standing flowers" in the center of the vase) became a popular form of flower arranging among the samurai class and aristocracy.

In 1462, Ikenobo Senkei—the Buddhist priest of Kyoto Rokkakudo—appeared in historical records as "master of flower arranging," so he is considered the one who established the philosophy and technique of Ikebana.

Around the Momoyama period (1568–1600), side by side with the rapidly expanding Tatebana style of flower artistry, came Chabana ("tea flowers"), an additional component of the art of Ikebana. Chabana (an element related to Ikebana's rich history), refers specifically to the flower display in the room or space for chadō (the tea ceremony), and though it is fundamentally a form of Ikebana, it comprises a genre of its own.

A simplified Nageire ("throw-in") style of Ikebana also appeared, in the wabi-sabi spirit (which means finding beauty in nature's imperfections) and was connected with Zen philosophy.

The Ikenobo style of Tatebana refined its style to Rikka (which interestingly is also translated as "standing flowers"). While Rikka became popular among wealthy townspeople, the need for a more simplified and dignified style of Ikebana arose in the mid-eighteenth century, resulting in the formalization of the Shoka or Seika ("fresh flowers") style, which is classical in appearance but asymmetrical in structure.

With Meiji period (1868–1912) modernization, the art of Ikebana became open to women. The Meiji government had a goal of educating women to become "good wives and wise mothers" and, as part of this character formation, Ikebana—once a male art form—became a standard part of women's education. This established the basis for the revival of Ikebana and, in one generation, made it pass from being a male practice to one open to women.

The introduction of Western culture to Japan was bound to affect flower arranging, and it did. In the late nineteenth century, Ohara Unshin popularized the Moribana ("piled-up flowers") style of Ikebana, which was incorporated the new Western flowers available for Ikebana arrangements. Moribana style uses a shallow container and a kenzan, or spiky floral frog, to support the stems. Much freer in approach than the Shoka style, Moribana rapidly became the most popular form of all.

When it was generally believed that practicing Ikebana meant following established forms, Teshigahara Sofu recognized Ikebana as a creative art and founded the Sogetsu School in 1927. Sofu believed that creative Ikebana (freestyle arranging) should be the mainstream of Ikebana, which gave a breath of fresh air to the Ikebana world. The school was one of the first to have textbooks written in English, which further expanded those who could learn the art.

There are now about three hundred schools that teach Ikebana all over the world, but the three major schools, which are characterized by a modern and free style, are Ikenobo, Ohara-ryu, and Sogetsu-ryu.

Modern Ikebana

When I tried to arrange flowers in the Ikebana style for the very first time, I immediately fell in love with the art of creating beautiful, minimalistic floral arrangements. I found it similar to painting or to creating sculpture. Even with small amounts of materials (about three to ten stems), I learned to make dynamic, yet poetic, arrangements. Of course, with more flowers and foliage, one can create gorgeous arrangements too. From minimal to abundant, Ikebana is very flexible and efficient, and there is very little waste. Flowers can be used from the time they bud, through flowering, and even after withering. Using the plants through their entire life cycle brings joy and honor to them.

In the following pages, I introduce the necessary techniques needed to create Ikebana, from simple to complex arrangements.

When I started learning Ikebana, I was taught to internally "dialogue" with flowers, to be aware of the space, to think visually and ask myself intentional questions such as "Which angle of flower looks more attractive?" and "How long a stem will be perfect in this space?" I was instructed to use my intuition and to intentionally and mindfully follow my feelings. This is how I learned to connect with my inner self and follow my instincts.

I become the medium for the expression of what nature offers. It brings peace to my mind, and it can do the same for you. When I am doing Ikebana, I feel like I'm meditating. This Japanese practice is not only delicately beautiful, but it also gives the silent and fulfilling experience of creating interactive art.

Ikebana is something you can spend a lifetime with because the simple botanical aesthetic has a deep and complex beauty. By using your senses and feelings, your creations will become a reflection of your spirit and state of mind. So even your first attempts at Ikebana are precious, beautiful, and loveable. You will surely find your own original style.

Basic Principles of Ikebana

Early Ikebana created by Buddhist monks included nine key positions of botanicals within the arrangement. Each element was intended to symbolize the perfect beauty of paradise, and as a result, the arrangements were often both complex and ornate.

The nine placements of the botanicals included elements that represented the spiritual mountain, receiving, waiting, an element representing a waterfall, a supporting branch, a stem that represented a stream, another to represent an overlook, and then two to represent both the front and back of the body.

While modern Ikebana is not so regimented, there are some traditions that have remained an important part of the practice.

State of Mind

Before you begin creating Ikebana, it is important to allow the stresses of life to fall away because Ikebana isn't just putting together floral arrangements—it's allowing yourself to commune with the flowers themselves, the space you are occupying, and the aesthetic you are creating. Here is a list of how you should approach your time creating Ikebana.

1. Begin with a clear mind; be serene and calm. Solitary time becomes rich when working on this art form.

2. Be mindful of connecting with your heart. Your Ikebana is a reflection of your soul.

3. Be careful and intentional with your preparation and then take care of the finished arrangement.

4. Communicate with the flowers as you arrange them. To do so, observe the flowers carefully to find their charm or uniqueness. Turn them to see all angles to help you make a decision about how to place them in the arrangement.

5. Keep the area around the vase clean and tidy even while arranging the flowers. It helps to keep your mind clear.

Creation Tips: Mass, Line, Color

There are three main elements to consider when creating Ikebana. These are mass, line, and color, as well as the interaction between them. The placement of each element will give a sense of movement, balance, and harmony.

Mass refers to the density of materials within the arrangement. How close together they are and how much space is between the blooms and stems creates an emphasis, and sometimes a focal point, within the arrangement.

Line refers to the sculptural element created by the branches and stems, as well with the space around them. The branches and stems used in Ikebana are as important as the flowers because they create visual structure and rhythm. The idea is to be minimalist and asymmetrical while creating balanced harmony. In Ikebana arrangements, the flowers are often put into place at angles, unlike Western designs which usually contain flowers arranged vertically in vases. Most Ikebana uses a minimal number of flowers.

Color is also an important fundamental to consider when practicing the art of Ikebana. The decision you will have to make is whether you want to create an arrangement with colors that are in harmony with each other or are contrasting with each other. You can determine whether colors are complementary or contrasting by consulting a color wheel. The closer colors are to each other on the wheel, the more they are in harmony. If they are across from each other on a color wheel, they are contrasting. You can also create Ikebana using only one color.

Flow is to create a sense of connection between the each floral materials to give harmony to the overall arrangement. Try to arrange quickly, before you have a chance to overthink the placement, but remember to pay attention to each bloom so you can determine which way it will be most beautiful before placing it.

I will go into more detail about these concepts later in this chapter, but for now, keep these tips in mind:

- To create a sense of movement, arrange floral materials of different lengths and in different directions.

- If you find yourself confused and lost when designing arrangements, try to remove one or two floral materials. Most of the time, you will see what to place next. Remember that leaves can be trimmed off if you need to create more space.

- Be aware not only of height and width, but also of depth, which will add a story to your arrangement and make the difference between a simple design and a more sophisticated one.

- Be aware of the harmony between the flowers, the vase, and the place. Dull Ikebana lacks the dynamics of rhythm, density, and emphasis.

- To create a graceful balance and a tight arrangement, align the bottoms of the stems.

- While you are creating your arrangement, view it from different sides and try to look at it with an objective eye.

- Cultivate an eye for appreciation and a hand for creation. A sense of balance is essential. This can be achieved through constant practice.

Essential Tools for Ikebana

There are a few essential tools you will want to have on hand to help stabilize the floral materials you will use to create Ikebana.

I normally use basic tools only, such as a pair of scissors and a kenzan (also known as a floral frog), but I do sometimes use saws or wires when creating larger arrangements. However, for most Ikebana, as long as I have a pair of scissors and a three-inch kenzan, I can create most of my arrangements. So for beginners, those are the only two essential items.

Because Ikebana is about creating inner peace as well as creating beautiful arrangements, it is important to enter into the art with a clear, serene mind. Keeping the tools clean and treating them with good care will help you reset your mind and clear away any distractions. So before you begin, align your thoughts. Also, by tidying up your Ikebana workspace, you will find calm which will help you find inspiration.

An assortment of kenzan. There are various sizes and materials.

Kenzan is a flower frog, and it is a must-have tool for Ikebana. It is composed of a heavy lead plate covered in sharp pins. Its pins pierce through the bases of the stems to hold them in the desired position. Nowadays, kenzan are not only for Ikebana arrangers. They are becoming more popular among florists and flower lovers everywhere.

The most common shape is round, and the most useful size is approximately three inches in diameter, which is what I use most often. If you only want to buy one kenzan, get this size.

A bigger kenzan is better for a larger arrangement, to hold more and heavier floral materials. A smaller kenzan is better for a compact vase. A black kenzan is best for a dark-colored vase.

The "oasis" (floral foam) that Western florists use is not recommended for Ikebana because the foam does not allow the angles of the plants to be readjusted. Plus, the used oasis becomes unrecyclable trash in the end; so over time, it is quite a large waste. So from the point of view of environmental protection, using a kenzan is becoming ever more popular among florists as well as people who practice Ikebana at home.

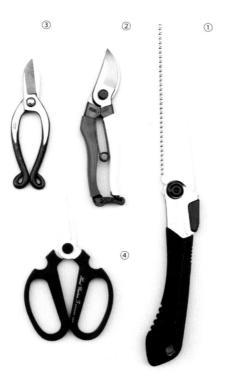

You will also need something to cut stems. Here is a list of the most commonly used tools for cutting:

1. A folding saw to cut thick, woody branches

2. Hand pruners to cut thinner branches

3. Classic Ikebana scissors to cut stems

4. Large loop-handled scissors for comfort of use

All cutting tools should be cleaned and dried with a cloth soon after use.

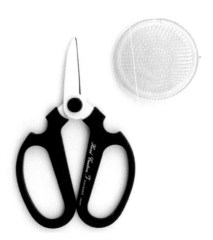

Floral wires and pliers are occasionally used as well. I use brown wire to safely fix the branches together in place when needed, especially when making large arrangements. The green wire is mainly used for the green stems. Pliers are useful for twisting the wire neatly.

And of course, scissors and a kenzan are a must.

These scissors, made in Japan by Sakagen, are comfortable to use and cut very well. The blade is coated with fluoride, so it is resistant to rust and very easy to maintain.

A plastic kenzan is often used for glass vase arrangements or centerpiece arrangements, because it becomes almost invisible in water. However, it is not very heavy, so it is only effective for light floral materials.

If you have these tools, you are on your way to creating a beautiful Ikebana arrangement.

I prefer to use the classic steel scissors because I love the crisp, clear sound they make when they cut the floral materials. The cloth is used to keep the area around my vase clean and tidy while arranging flowers. It helps me clear my mind to get better inspiration.

This is an indispensable Ikebana kenzan accessory with a reversible, dual-use tool to repair and clean the kenzan needles.

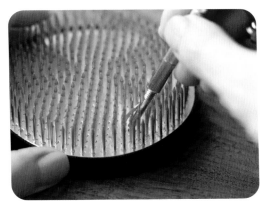

When you cut floral stems, do so in water to prolong their life and beauty. Be sure to always cut every single stem in water. This will renew the section of the stem that is dirty with bacteria and make it easier for the stem to absorb water.

The thin needles of the kenzan often get bent when using hard, woody materials. Insert the tube side of this tool into the bent needle and raise it vertically.

The Moribana Style

Learning the basics of Moribana (which means piled-up flowers) is the first step to mastering the skill of creating beautiful Ikebana arrangements. A major feature of Moribana is using a kenzan in a shallow vase. In this lesson, I will show you some basic styles using this important technique. Although this is an Ikebana basic, these types of arrangements contain a beautiful balance and harmony. I still often create floral arrangements using this basic style.

I like to start students who are new to Ikebana with Moribana, not only because it's a building block to the art, but also because it's how I began. I still remember the quiet excitement of the moment I opened the door to this new world of Ikebana.

Mastering the use of a kenzan is important. If you don't master the technique, not only will the arrangement lose its shape on the way, but you will also not be able to incorporate the inspiration that comes into the arrangement. To put it in other words, if you master these techniques, you will be able to fully demonstrate your own free expression. And using a kenzan is very fun, so please enjoy it.

How to Use the Kenzan to Hold and Stabilize Floral Materials

As I noted in the "Tools" section, the kenzan is the most popular and useful tool for stabilizing floral materials. They come in a variety of sizes, shapes, and materials. Your vase size will determine which kenzan to use. I mostly use a round, three-inch-diameter kenzan in brass.

How to Stabilize Regular Stems

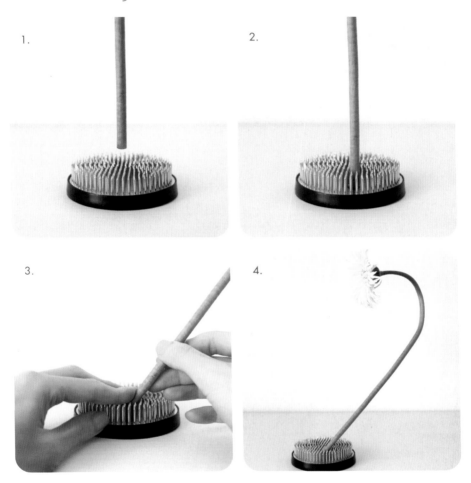

1. Flower and leaf stems are usually soft and easy to insert into a kenzan, so cut them straight.

2. Insert the stem firmly into the bottom of the kenzan.

3. To make an angle, first insert the stem straight and then gradually tilt it, but keep holding the bottom of the stem and pushing it in the direction you want to tilt it. If you hold the middle of the stem and tilt it down, the stem will break.

4. The stem was fixed firmly at the desired angle.

How to Stabilize Thin Stems

1.

2.

3.

4.

1.   If the stem is thinner than the space between the needles of the kenzan, it will not be firmly fixed into the kenzan.

2.   Insert it into a thicker stem to make the base thicker.

3.   Wrap it with extra stems with wire to reinforce it.

4.   Wrap it with paper to reinforce it. No tape is needed.

How to Stabilize Branches

1. Most branches have solid, hard stalks that are difficult to push into the kenzan needles, so cut them diagonally to insert them more easily.

2. When inserting a branch into the kenzan, hold the branch firmly with both hands and insert it deep into the kenzan. If it is inserted too shallowly, the branch will not be stable.

3. Make sure to insert the branch all the way to the bottom of the kenzan so that it doesn't lose its form in the middle; then you can calmly focus on your arrangement.

4. To make an angle, first insert the branch straight and then gradually tilt it, but keep holding the bottom of the branch with your hand and pushing it in the direction you want to tilt it in.

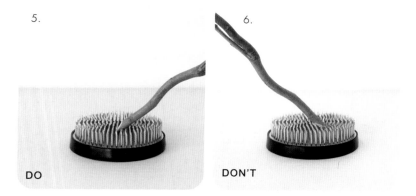

5. When the branch is fixed at an angle, cut it, leaving the bark on the side where the branch will incline.

6. Tilting the side with no bark left; the branch will not be stable.

How to Stabilize Thick Branches

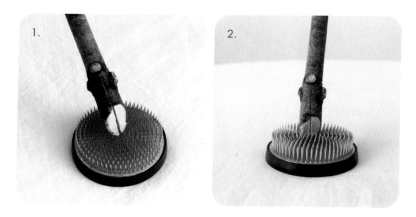

1. For thicker branch stalks, cut the stalk diagonally first, then cut the middle of the stalk and split it into thinner stalks. In this way, it is much easier to insert the branch into a kenzan's needles and stabilize it.

2. Straighten up the branch and insert it deeply into the kenzan with both hands. To make an angle, gradually tilt it while holding the bottom part of the branch.

How to Balance Heavy Floral Materials

Certain floral materials, especially large, tilting branches with many leaves, may be too top-heavy for a kenzan to support. If even a large kenzan can't support them, place another kenzan upside down and use it as a stabilizer weight.

Moribana Style Tutorials

Upright-Style Moribana
Materials: Gladiolus, Dahlia, Dusty Miller and Ruscus

All basic moribana arrangements begin with a triangle framework. To create this structure, you will need three different flower lengths or "lines": tall line, middle line, and short line. To begin, arrange the flowers by poking the stems into the spikes of the kenzan. Leave space between the stems so that it creates a three-dimensional triangle, with the point of the triangle directed into the kenzan.

The different stem lengths create a sense of movement in the arrangement. Once the three-dimensional space is completed, add more flower stems to build a beautiful, dramatic arrangement. Ikebana creates a well-balanced space based on the relationship between materials and vases, so the lengths of the stems are determined by the size of the vase.

If your vase is small, cut down the stems to an appropriate length, otherwise your arrangement will look awkward. On the other hand, if your vase is big, do not cut the stems too short, or the vase will be the focal point of your arrangement.

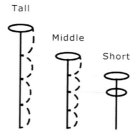

Approximate length of stems:

Tall line = "The size of vase" x 1.5–2
Middle line = ¾ of Tall line
Short line = ¾ or ½ of Middle line

This length guide is a standard for any basic style. These are the lengths of the floral material coming out of the vase. The most suitable size will be determined by the shape of the arrangement, the type of flowers or branches, and where the arrangement is to be placed.

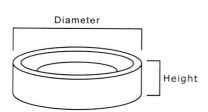

The size of vase = Diameter + Height

Place a kenzan in the corner of a vase to create "negative space." For more about "negative space," please see page 95.

Fill the vase with water until the kenzan is fully covered. Make a framework with three lines: tall line, middle line, and short line. Insert them to a kenzan in order from tallest to shortest. Arrange them so that the three lines create a three-dimensional triangle.

Above is a side view of the arrangement. In this arrangement, the tall line is leaning slightly backward, the middle line is leaning forward, and the short line is leaning close to the bottom. These three lines' height, width, and depth, create the three-dimensional triangle space.

In this arrangement, the short line of dahlia creates a bold angle, and this angle is what makes Ikebana unique and dramatic.

Insert the three lines so that they form a large triangle on the kenzan. You can add more stems later in the remaining space on the kenzan.

Insert additional stems to fill the space. Be careful not to put these stems higher than the

middle line. This way, your arrangement will be well organized and keep the three-dimensional space beautiful.

To make your arrangement look unique, insert the flowers asymmetrically.

Finally, place some dusty miller to finish your arrangement. A bare kenzan in a container doesn't look good, so hide the kenzan with floral materials if possible.

Once you have your flowers in place, step back and objectively observe your arrangement from a short distance. It will look quite different from how it looks up close. Once you have observed it from afar, go back and make fine adjustments, then step back and look again. Continue to go through that process until you are pleased with the arrangement.

Note: Arrange with your whole body, not just your hands.

Slanting-Style Moribana

Materials: Rosemary, Chrysanthemum, Statice and Ruscus

Compared to the Upright Style Moribana, in Slanting Style Moribana, the tall line is slightly tilted, giving the arrangement a softer feeling. The short line is also tilted low, creating a well-balanced space.

The composition and the fragrant rosemary give this arrangement a soothing effect.

First, place a kenzan in the corner of a vase to create "negative space." Fill the vase with water until the kenzan is fully covered. Make a framework with three lines: tall line, middle line, and short line. Insert them into the kenzan in order from tallest to shortest.

Insert the three lines so that they form a large triangle on the kenzan. You can easily add more stems into the remaining space later.

If you use a dark colored vase, a black kenzan is best.

Place more chrysanthemums in a low position with varying heights and angles. Then add a few stems for a pop of color.

Lastly, position some ruscus for the final effect.

> **Tip:** Place the front floral materials at a
> forward-facing angle to show their faces,
> rather than standing upward. By doing
> so properly, your arrangement will be
> stunning. Most inexperienced students have
> a hard time doing this, and I teach this tip
> over and over again in my classes.

As you can see, the floral materials create
a smooth flow between the three lines, and
the stems in the back give this arrangement a
sense of depth.

> **Note:** In Ikebana, creating a sense of
> depth is an important element, because
> the perception of depth adds interest to
> the arrangement. Use of depth is one main
> difference between beginner-level and
> advanced-level skill mastery.

Slanting-Style Moribana, Second Tutorial

Materials: Grevillea, Alstroemeria and Ruscus

Place a kenzan at the left corner of the vase. Fill the vase with water until the kenzan is fully covered.

Trim and add two grevillea flowers as the tall and middle lines. Add one stem of alstroemeria as the short line to create the three-dimensional space. Insert the stems in order, from tallest to shortest.

Add more stems of alstroemeria and ruscus to fill the space and hide the kenzan. To create depth, the flowers and leaves in the back should be leaning backward.

The mass created by the alstroemeria and ruscus in the lower center gives stability to this wide-open composition. The tall line and middle line are widely separated in this arrangement, so the depth and the width of the open space can be emphasized.

Vase Techniques

If you have ever seen an Ikebana arrangement in a tall, narrow vase, it was most likely created in the Nageire style. In contrast to the Moribana style, which is lower and wider and uses a kenzan, the Nageire style is a vertically or horizontally oriented arrangement that often uses a narrow-mouthed, tall vase without a kenzan. In Ikebana, Nageire is as common as Moribana.

It's a good idea to decide in advance where you intend to place your flower arrangement, and then choose whether to make it Moribana or Nageire.

Since it does not use a kenzan, the techniques for creating Nageire are different from Moribana. Because the flower materials move easily in the vase, it is necessary to devise a way to stabilize them, so in this section, I will show you techniques such as how to create a "cross-bar fixture," a "vertical-type fixture," or a "direct fixture," as well as how to bend branches. Through practice, you will learn to easily "fix" or stabilize the flowers using the above techniques, which will allow you to arrange them faster. But don't worry if it is a slow process in the beginning. Going slowly and reflecting on each placement is an important part of creating Ikebana. As you become more experienced, your "performance" will become faster.

For beginners, I recommend a narrow-mouthed (3½-to-4-inch mouth) vase. The smaller the vase's diameter, the easier it is to use, because it requires less flower material and is easier to arrange. Once you get used to creating arrangements in vases with small diameters, you can move up to creating Ikebana in larger vases.

Compared to Moribana, there are many more vases to choose from in Nageire, and the combination of vases and flowers can greatly expand the variety of arrangements.

How to Fix Materials

Branches and stems are fixed, or held in place, without any utensils such as a kenzan in the Nageire style. There are three important methods of fixing the branches and stems. Each has its own features; choose the most suitable method depending on the composition, the materials, or the vase to be used.

Cross-Bar Fixtures

Crossbars are made with two pieces of cut-off branches. The branch has to be hard enough to create this form. This method puts a lot of force on the vase, so thin, delicate, or precious vases are not suitable for this method of stabilization.

Cut one end diagonally and the other end straight.

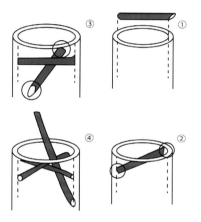

1. Both pieces are cut to a little longer than the inside diameter of the vase. One side is slanted, and the other side is straight.

2. Hold the end of the first cut piece lower than the rim of the vase, with its slanted cut end facing down.

3. The second piece is pulled up with its slanted cut end facing upward.

4. Place the floral materials at your desired angle. If the materials don't stay in place well, bend them slightly to achieve a good balance.

The ends of the branches that are cut at an angle bend slightly to fit the wall of the vase.

A view of the cross-bar fixture from above. In addition, to stabilize a branch more firmly with this cross-bar fixture, bending the branch slightly will help balance it well.

Vertical Fixtures

This method can be used as long as the branches are thick and strong enough for splitting.

With a vertical-type fixture, branches can be fixed at the ideal angle. I often use this fixture to stabilize a branch that could not be fixed with other fixture methods.

1. The upright branch of the fixture is split and should be slightly shorter than the height of the vase.

2. Split the main branch equally in half as well.

3. Interlock the fixture and the main branch, and then place them in the vase.

4. When their ends touch the circle parts, they will be securely fixed.

A view of the vertical-type fixture from above.

Material: Blueberry branch
Vase: tomoro pottery

The arrangement was completed using a
vertical-type fixture. The second branch is
placed low on the left side of the vase by
interlocking it with the fixture and the main stem
which is already fixed.

Direct Fixing

In this method, a branch is fixed at two points: at the inner wall of the vase and at the rim of the vase. By fixing these two points, the branch will be stable. If there are more than two branches, arrange them so that they cross to interlock and support each other in the vase. If the branches are too straight, it will be difficult to balance them. In that case, bend them slightly to make them easier to keep in balance.

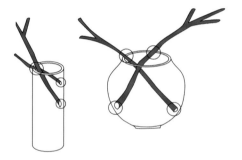

Arrange branches in such a way that they eventually cross inside the vase and support each other. When a branch touches the two circled points, it will be stable. If you're using more than two branches, arrange them to interlock and support each other, so that they will be fixed more securely.

Though this is the easiest of the three fixing methods, you will need some practice to fix all the materials and create your desired arrangement. Bending the branch will increase its stability.

A view of direct fixing from above.

Cutting and Fixing

In Nageire, all the ends of the materials should be cut on a slant, so that they firmly press the inside wall of the vase. The materials are placed in the vase in such a way that the cut ends stick to the inner wall of the vase for balancing, not to the bottom of the vase.

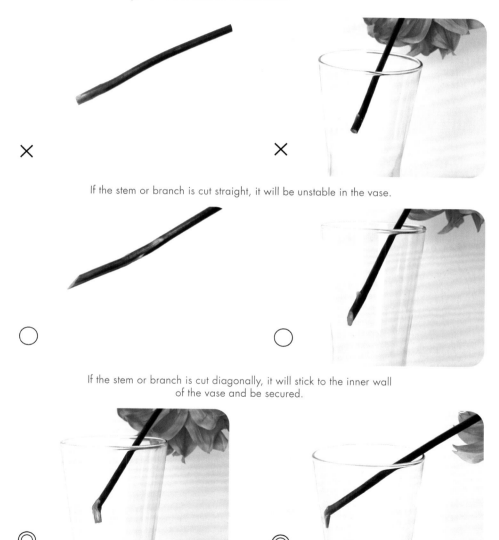

If the stem or branch is cut straight, it will be unstable in the vase.

If the stem or branch is cut diagonally, it will stick to the inner wall of the vase and be secured.

A large flower especially has heavy heads, so crush the cut ends of the stem with your fingers to make it stick to the walls of the vase easier and more firmly.

DON'T

DO

In principle, in the Nageire style of Ikebana, the floral materials don't touch the bottom of the vase except in some special cases, because they will only be facing upward, which doesn't create beautiful movements in the arrangement.

Angle the stems of floral materials to create flexible movements in the arrangement, such as turning the flowers' faces forward or varying their heights. The stems stick to the wall of the vase to hold them in place. You can see that the stems are not touching the bottom of the vase in the photo.

I added branches and leaves to complete the arrangement.

Bending Technique

Before bending, check the front and back of the branch to make sure the front side is facing forward, and then decide the position to place it in. The front of the branch is the side with more flowers or fruits, the side whose leaves exhibit movement that most resembles movement toward the sun, or, if there are no crucial elements, the side whose movement is toward the front.

You need to observe your floral material carefully to find its best beauty every time you place it in a vase. By placing the branch to face the front, your arrangement will have an energetic and lively look.

Plants grow cheerfully toward the sun, so that is the front of the plants. Keep in mind that, for branches with flowers, the direction in which most flowers are facing is the front side. For branches without flowers, the direction in which most leaves are facing is the front side.

Front side. The flowers are facing the viewer. Use this side for the arrangement.

Back side. The flowers are facing away.

How to Bend Branches

1. Before bending.

2. To bend a branch, put your fingers close together while applying pressure slowly. If you are not sure how flexible the branch is, try it with an extra branch first.

3. After bending. A nice, smooth curve was created without breaking the branch.

How to Bend Stems

1. Before bending.

2. Gently apply pressure to create a curve in the stem.

3. When bending a stem, add a slight twist to make a beautiful line without folding or breaking it.

4. After bending. The stem line becomes soft and refined.

Nageire Style Tutorials

Upright Style Nageire

Materials: Japanese Fantail Willow, Anemone, and Ruscus

Just like basic Moribana style, all basic Nageire arrangements begin with a three-dimensional triangle framework. So you will need three different "lines" or lengths of flowers or branches: tall line, middle line, and short line. The different lengths of materials will create a sense of movement. In this arrangement, the tall line is the longest Japanese fantail willow, the middle line is the shorter stem of Japanese fantail willow placed in front of the tall line, and the short line is the anemone on the far left.

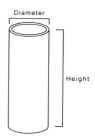

The size of vase = Diameter + Height

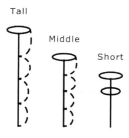

Approximate length of stems:

Tall line = "The size of vase" x 1.5–2
Middle line = ¾ of Tall line
Short line = ¾ or ½ of Middle line

This length guide is a standard for any basic style. These are the lengths of the floral materials coming out of the vase. The most suitable size will be decided by the shape of the arrangement, the condition of materials, and where the arrangement is to be placed.

From the top view, you can clearly see the three-dimensional space. In the middle of three-dimensional structure, two stems of anemone and ruscus leaves are added for balance.

Make a framework with three lines: tall line, middle line, and short line. Insert them in the vase using fixtures, in order from tallest to shortest.

Arrange them with enough space so the stems are not too far and not too close.

Add the anemone in a low angle.

Fill the middle space with two stems of anemone. Place them asymmetrically, in different lengths and directions to give the arrangement a sense of natural movement. Face one of the anemones forward so that the overall arrangement looks lively.

This arrangement is perfect to try the "one bar fixture" because the mouth of the vase is small. After making the fixture, fill the vase with water to make it stable.

To finish up, position some ruscus leaves to fill in the middle spaces between the stems. Don't forget to add in the material on the back side of the vase, which adds depth to the arrangement.

Slanting-Style Nageire
Materials: Pussy Willow, Rose and Ruscus

In this arrangement, the tall line is the longest pussy willow, the middle line is a shorter stem of pussy willow, and the short line is the rose on the right side.

The green leaves create a smooth flow by connecting each stem together. Although leaves are not the main materials, they do give a dramatic effect.

From this angle you can see how open and dynamic the three-dimensional space is.

Choose which fixture technique you would like to use and then create the fixture from the branches. In this arrangement, I used both the "cross-bar fixture" and "vertical-type fixture" because the tall branch can be difficult to fix with just a cross-bar fixture. You can always mix several techniques in Ikebana.

After making the fixture, fill the vase with water. This will make the vase more stable.

Create a framework with three lines: a tall line, a middle line, and a short line. Insert them in the vase using fixtures, in order from tallest to shortest.

Arrange them at a certain distance, not too far or too close. Those three lines will create three-dimensional triangle space.

> **Note:** If you don't have any nice looking branches, you can create an attractive line by combining a few branches. You can also add branches to create volume.

When using a cross-bar fixture, stems can be fixed at any angle. The ends of the stem should be cut at an angle in the Nageire style. The stems should firmly touch the inside wall of the vase. Usually, stems don't touch the bottom of the vase; instead they stick to the inner wall of the vase.

Add two more roses to fill the middle space. Place the flower faces in different directions to give your arrangement a natural, airy look. The different lengths of flowers will create a sense of movement within the arrangement. Once the three-dimensional triangle space is complete, add more flowers to make the best use of the space. Be sure to add the flowers in one at a time and then assess the arrangement after each flower has been placed.

At this point, be careful not to use stems that stick out too far from the three-dimensional triangle space, as they will break the flow by leaving no negative space.

Continue to add in more blooms until you feel that you have achieved the aesthetic you want. Insert your flowers asymmetrically to create sharp variation.

Objectively observe your arrangement from a short distance. You will find that it looks quite different from when you view it at a close distance. You will probably find that you want to make small adjustments. If so, make them and then repeat the process until you are pleased with the look.

Place some ruscus leaves to finish your arrangement. Try to connect each stem with ruscus to create a harmonious flow.

Whether branches or flowers, cut all the materials diagonally. In this arrangement, stems are fixed without any utensils like a kenzan.

Slanting-Style Nageire, Second Tutorial

Materials: Camellia Branch, Hypericum, Calla Lily and Aster

In comparison to the previous basic Nageire styles, this arrangement uses more varieties of botanicals. Still, its composition is simple: create a three-dimensional triangle space with three lines and then fill the empty space in the middle without breaking the three-dimensional triangle space.

In this arrangement, the tall line is a camellia branch on the left side, the middle line is red hypericum on the right side, and the short line is red hypericum, but arranged low in the front.

To begin, choose which fixture technique you would like to use and then create the fixture from branches. (The cross-bar fixture is applied in this arrangement.) Fill the vase with water and insert the three lines in the vase using a fixture, in order from tallest to shortest.

You can clearly see that the empty space in the middle has been filled. Additionally, the leaves sticking out in the back create depth.

Add two stems of calla lily in different lengths and directions to create movement. Make sure not to use long stems that stick out too far from the three-dimensional triangle space, as they will break the sense of negative space.

Place several aster stems in a low position in the middle to fill the space.

To finish up, insert a few stems of camellia leaves around middle line of red hypericum to give the arrangement a sense of harmonious flow and volume. Once again, don't forget to create depth, so place one stem of camellia on the back side.

Hanging Style Nageire

Materials: Rose and Raspberry Branch

Hanging style is one of the unique Nageire styles. In this arrangement, the tall line is arranged leaning downward from the vase to the table. Bold angles make a striking shape. To create this bold angle, choose a branch that is soft or can be bent. Carefully remove the excess leaves to expose the quality of the line.

You can stabilize the branches with a "cross-bar fixture."

Once the three-dimensional space is done, continue to add in more blooms until you feel that you have achieved your desired aesthetic. Flowers are placed not only in the front but also in the back to create a sense of depth and volume.

A raspberry branch is soft and suitable for this style. The tall line of the raspberry branch is bent to create a hanging style. For bending technique, please see page 48.

Clear Glass Vase Techniques

Transparent glass vases are often used in Ikebana, so intentional arrangement is important. Because the vase is transparent, it is important to keep the inside beautifully organized, so that your arrangement has a neat and clean look. Glass vase Ikebana arrangements have a fresh, seasonal look—especially during spring and summer.

When I use glass vases, I love to submerge some greens to give my arrangement a natural look. Even in water, these arrangements are long-lasting, and the green color makes it come alive. It's fun to transform a simple glass vase into a leaf pattern. In addition to leaves, I also use branches, such as cedarwood or curly willow, to create nice patterns.

If you have a shallow glass vase, you can use a kenzan for your arrangement. Because the kenzan is visible, you will want to either have an attractive kenzan or to obscure it with leaves or flower materials to create a natural-looking arrangement. If the flower material is light in weight, you can use a clear plastic kenzan, and then you don't have to be worried about hiding it.

Glass vases come in a variety of shapes and sizes and are reasonably priced. So once you have mastered this technique, you will be able to create endless Multi-Glass-Vase arrangements for any occasion. For Multi-Vase arrangements, please see page 86.

Clear Glass Vase Tutorials

Ikebana with Vines
Materials: Pandorea Vine, Lisianthus, and Bupleurum

The pandorea vine appears to dance in the water, emphasizing the characteristics of the glass vase in this arrangement. Green floral materials are used to express the freshness and coolness of early summer. By using one color, all lines of the material look connected and appear as a smooth overall flow.

Fill the vase with water. Trim the pandorea vines and submerge them in the water. Next, drape a nice curved pandorea vine outside the vase. Place some lisianthus and bupleurum together and rest them on the left rim of the vase.

Place the ends of the stems together, so that the inside of the vase is beautifully organized.

Because the vase is transparent, creating a simple, clean composition is key.

The stems need to be cut diagonally so that they firmly touch the wall of the vase.

A Small Glass Arrangement

Materials: Cornflower, Delphinium, and
Snow-on-the-Mountain

This is a small and easy arrangement using lightweight botanicals, so a clear plastic kenzan can be used. First, place a handful of snow-on-the-mountain on the plastic kenzan, then insert a cornflower and delphinium. Add one stem of cornflower to create a modest movement.

Small arrangements can be placed in a limited space. It is also nice to decorate the table with several small identical arrangements scattered around the table.

Glass Bowl Arrangement
Materials: Casablanca and Camellia Leaf

Casablanca flowers are gorgeous, so I normally use a tall vase for them. However, I tried the low glass bowl for this arrangement and was pleased with the results!

A plastic kenzan is placed at the right side of the vase. I placed the Casablanca flowers in the water playfully and low at various lengths and in different directions. The lines of the Casablanca leaves also add movement. If the arrangement has too many lines, trim the leaves to create space.

Add camellia leaves to create a beautiful composition from all angles.

Arrangement in a Square Glass Vase

Materials: Globe Amaranth, Rose, Scabiosa, Ruscus, and Oriental Bittersweet Leaves

This is useful as a vase because it has a smooth surface and an opening that is perfect for embellishing flowers. The glass block is also heavy enough to hold the tall branches.

After placing globe amaranth and ruscus in the vase, add a rose and a scabiosa on the right side. In this case, a kenzan is not necessary. Then, place two stems of oriental bittersweet leaves flowing upward. It should look like the globe amaranth is trying to climb out of the vase. It creates a botanical garden with a story.

Using pink bonbon-like flowers to decorate the inside of a glass vase gives the arrangement a pretty touch! Add ruscus leaves to make the bottom of the arrangement look beautiful as well.

Globe amaranth is a long-lasting fresh-cut flower and it is an excellent dried flower that retains color well.

Dainty Glass Arrangement
Materials: Dahlia, Baby's Breath, and Lily Grass

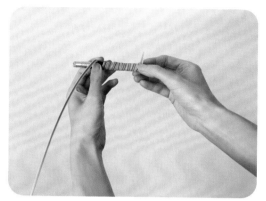

Dainty like a wedding arrangement, the look is one of pureness and serenity. The lily grasses are made into heart-shaped curves like ribbons on the left side of the arrangement. The two stems of dahlia look like a couple cuddling.

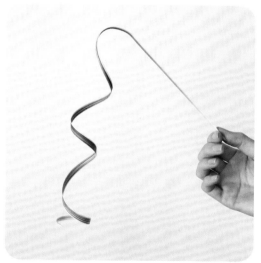

To add a curved line to the lily grass, wrap it around a pen or pencil. Hold them together for about ten seconds then unwrap the lily grass. It will look like a curly ribbon. It's very easy!

You can see the lines of lily grass are luxuriously and gently intertwined. A kenzan is not necessary.

Arrangement in a Glass Candleholder

Materials: Miniature Sunflower, Ivy, and Lily Grass

I found a tiny sunflower at a farmer's market, so I decided to use a glass candleholder as a vase for it. I arranged the sunflower with ivy and lily grass. I was delighted to find that a candleholder can be a perfect vase for tiny wildflowers.

I used lily grass to add straight and curved lines. Introducing "mass" and "line" creates simple, yet very sophisticated arrangements.

The lily grasses are arranged at the end to balance the overall arrangement.

Narrow Vase Arrangement

Materials: Pink Snowberry, Spray Rose, and Curly Willow

This is a dainty arrangement in a delicate glass vase. To avoid making the inside of the vase look messy and dirty, cut the stems short, leaving only the curly willow branches long.

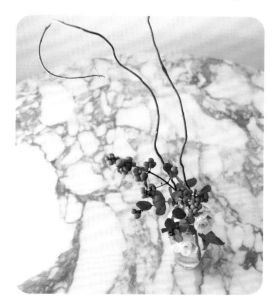

The leaves are also placed on the back side to create depth, giving the entire arrangement a good balance.

The mouth of the vase is very narrow, so the number of floral materials you can use is very limited. It is important to carefully consider each stem that you add to the arrangement. Luckily, with this type of the vase, it is very easy to stabilize your floral materials.

Narrow Vase Arrangement: Version 2

Materials: Camellia and Lily Grass

The same glass vase is used to create a refined, minimal arrangement. A mini camellia is added as a focal point. The short camellia and circle-shaped lily grass offers a contemporary look.

Favorite Flowers Arrangement
Materials: Dahlia, Blue Ice Cypress, and Viburnum Tinus

As you can see, this arrangement has a very simple composition. Only three stems of floral material are needed. Don't think too hard about this one: if you don't have access to the flowers suggested, simply combine your favorite botanicals with your favorite vase. All you have to do is relax and enjoy creating. Surround yourself with things you love—they will bring you quiet excitement and inspire you!

I love the color of blue ice cypress. It's very chic, so I picked them as a main material of this arrangement. I filled the glass vase with the blue ice cypress and made the cedar pattern vase. I added one stem of dahlia for a bright focal point.

Lastly, a few of the viburnum tinus berries were placed at the back of the arrangement to create variation.

Vase: Hasami Porcelain

This is another version of the arrangement, using the same materials in Moribana style with a kenzan.

Insert two branches of blue ice cypress in at different lengths, with one leaning forward and the other leaning slightly backward to create a gentle space. Place some blue ice cypress on top of the water on the left side of the vase to create a beautiful flow.

Finally, insert one stem of dahlia in a lower position as a vivid focal point.

The matte silver-green of the blue ice cypress and the matte black of the vase match well, creating a dramatic effect.

Branch Arrangement in Glass

Materials: Monstera, Snowball Viburnum, Ornithogalum, and Ruscus

This is a good example of an arrangement that uses "direct fixing" for the snowball viburnum. With monstera as a focal point, the branches are placed asymmetrically with different lengths on each side, and the V-shape creates negative space in the center of the arrangement. Without the negative space, it would lose its visual strength. When you arrange branches, remember to trim excess leaves and twigs. In this arrangement, most of the leaves have been carefully removed so that the flower parts of the snowball become more prominent.

To make your arrangement glorious, place the ornithogalum low in the middle.

Dried Flowers in Glass
Materials: Dried Rosehip and White Lysimachia

This vase is made of Bohemian crystal and it is one of my favorites. Dried branches of rosehip are the main focal point in this arrangement. The contrast between the beautiful vase and the aged, dried branches creates a sense of drama.

Because Ikebana is a spare flower arranging style, the vase is an important part of the artwork. By keeping the floral materials to a minimum, this arrangement maximizes the presence of the vase.

Remove any excess twigs to make the lines of the branch stand out.

It is a time-consuming process, but it makes a big difference in the finished result.

Before trimming

After trimming

Vase Collection Techniques

How many vases do you have? I'm sure that most of you have at least a couple, but if not, there are many charming vases in every color and price to be found in stores, and it can be nice to use them in multi-vase arrangements.

With two or more vases, you can make an opulent, gorgeous arrangement without needing a lot of flowers. In Ikebana, there are always new, surprising approaches to arranging flowers.

Using multiple vases to create one arrangement does not require any new techniques. You just need to be more conscious of the overall composition of your arrangement to create visual connections between vases. Making a multi-vase arrangement takes a little more time and effort, but the end result will be impressive.

With practice, you will learn to make connections and find rhythms within the multi-arrangements through the flow and the lines of your floral materials. This will allow you to create the illusion of one big arrangement and build a fluent conversation between the materials, as if the flowers are talking to each other. You can also connect the leaves to create fluidity. By following these tips, you can craft an endless flow of arrangements using as many vases as you want:

- Select vases of varying heights and sizes to give dimension to the overall composition.
- It is not always necessary to use the same type of vase. By using similar flower materials throughout, you can create a sense of unity between the different vases.
- Use the botanical materials to connect the vases visually to inspire harmony.
- Once you have created the Ikebana arrangements, place vases diagonally to create drama and expand the space, rather than placing them right next to each other.

Multi-Vase Arrangement

Materials: Ranunculus, Seeded Eucalyptus, Lily Grass, and Sage
Vase: Glass Vases

In this arrangement, ten stems of white ranunculus and a bit of greenery are arranged to create a dramatic floral display. Three small arrangements are visually tied together with lily grasses to create a smooth flow between vases.

You can create movement by varying the heights of the vases. Of course, varying the heights and directions of the flowers and greenery is necessary as well. The addition of sage completes the look.

This style is very flexible. It is great for wedding centerpieces because it can be a multitude of sizes, shapes, heights, and color palettes.

To highlight the inside of the glass vase, keep all the stems short except for the sage.

Place vases diagonally, rather than placing them right next to each other, to create depth and expand the space.

I don't use a lot of floral materials in this arrangement because the space between the botanicals and the vases makes it look large.

Dried Branch Arrangement

*Materials: French Marigold, Solidago,
Geranium Leaf, Seeded Eucalyptus, and Dried
Grapewood Branches*
Vase: Hasami Porcelain

This arrangement is best for special occasions, such as flower exhibitions or store displays. Different sizes of vases and dried grapewood branches vary the rhythms of the overall arrangement. The beige color adds a sense of unity.

Combining two or more of these arrangements can make a gorgeous visual statement even with just a few floral materials.

Coordinating the vases is also a fun process. Before you begin arranging, take some time to select vases that accentuate what you love most about your flowers. Amassing a small collection of vases will allow you to build a variety of arrangements.

Dramatic Dahlia Arrangement

Materials: Dahlia, Globe Amaranth, and
Curly Willow
Vase: Astier de Villatte

It's a pleasure for me to arrange such large, beautiful dahlias. I started arranging without a plan, but the flowers were so big that I decided to use two vases. This arrangement requires the use of a kenzan. Inspiration struck when I placed three stems of dahlia in each vase, and because it is a fairly simple arrangement, I thought it would be perfect to use as a tutorial.

This is a scene of a happy family: a small child is looking up at their mom and dad, and the parents are smiling at the child lovingly.

The curly willow branches and globe amaranth rising upward cheerfully express their joy. The arrangement became a story.

Christmas Ikebana

Materials: Narcissus, Pepperberry, Rosehip,
Silver Dollar Eucalyptus, and Spanish Moss
Vase: Simone Bodmer-Turner and
Marloe Marloe

This is a Christmas arrangement using two vases. Each vase is filled with a small amount of floral material, and the two are combined to create a big, festive Christmas display.

A stem of eucalyptus rising from the right side of the vase provides a sense of flow between the two arrangements. The Spanish moss plays an important role in connecting the two vases as well.

This contemporary object-like vase on the left side is also an attractive part of the arrangement.

The Christmas wreath was made of curly willow branches.

The pepper berry is arranged in a natural, casual way, but the excess leaves and twigs are trimmed away.

Understanding the Importance of Negative Space

"Space is the breath of art."
—Frank Lloyd Wright

In this lesson, I will teach you how to use space effectively by intentionally creating negative space in an arrangement. In Ikebana, the negative space is just as important as the elements that make up the arrangement itself. The flowers, branches, or foliage are the positive space or focal point, but the negative space plays an equally important role.

Negative space is the area between and around the elements (in the case of Ikebana, it is the space between flowers, stems, branches, or other objects in the arrangement). It is the area we generally think of as "empty."

The balance between negative and positive space is important in all types of art and design—whether it is a photographic composition, a painting, or an interior design. Negative space helps draw attention to the composition and allows the work of art to have balance and elegance. In most forms of art, the balance can be symmetrical or asymmetrical (or imperfect), as long as it is intentional. In Ikebana, however, one of the major characteristics of the art is asymmetrical (or imperfect) balance, because it adds to the drama of the arrangement. It is intentionally unbalanced and creates tension, so it is more eye-catching. The imbalance catches the viewer's attention and is engaging because one can't help but wonder how the arrangement is staying in place.

Adding negative space also creates additional drama. The arrangement will be more visually interesting and intriguing. Can't you feel the story? It gives a sense of tranquility and adds a romantic nature to the flowers. The simplicity that may give the impression of boredom at first glance becomes graceful. The effect becomes more potent and profound.

Although Ikebana is a traditional Japanese cultural practice that has been around for hundreds of years, it is very fresh and modern as well. Ikebana is a true and intentional form of contemporary minimalism and if we are intentional about where we place Ikebana arrangements, they will become contemporary objects as well as botanical arrangements. So while you are creating your Ikebana, it is important not only to pay attention to the positive space or focal point of the flowers themselves, but also to be conscious of the negative space.

Arrangement With
Negative Space

Arrangement Without Negative Space

Materials: Delphinium and Lisianthus

Here are examples of Moribana style with and without negative space. The difference is so obvious that you'll instantly understand the importance of negative space. The arrangements have the same materials, but they have different vibes—without the empty space, the arrangement is not compelling.

With a low, shallow, open vase like this one, the water becomes part of the scenery. Water is an important element in Ikebana; it is like there is a quiet, refreshing breeze blowing over the water.

*Materials: Balloon Milkweed, Snowberry,
and Delphinium*
Vase: tomoro pottery

For this arrangement, use the left side of the
vase for a more sophisticated look.

The kenzan is covered with white statice. You
might think that if you're going to hide it anyway,
you should use a smaller kenzan. However, most
small kenzans are not heavy enough to support
floral materials firmly. Small kenzans can only be
used when arranging light floral materials.

Arrangement With Negative Space

Materials: Curly Willow, Asclepias, and Obedient Plant
Vase: Alessi, Zaha Hadid design

Here is an example of an Ikebana arrangement using intentional negative space. I left the right half open to give the arrangement a powerful visual strength. The light pink obedient plants are placed so that they flow to the right, connecting with the branches and creating a smooth flow throughout the arrangement.

Arrangement Without Negative Space

Here is the same arrangement without using negative space. Although it isn't bad, it's not as sophisticated. When you feel something is missing in your arrangement, rather than adding more, one way to improve it is to create negative space.

The middle of the V-shaped branches can be considered negative space, but I removed all the branches on the right side to create negative space there as well.

Arrangement With Negative Space

The peony and pokeweed are placed on the right side of
the vase, effectively creating negative space on the left side.

Arrangement Without Negative Space

Here is the same arrangement without using negative space. Although it isn't bad, adding negative space provides an interesting feeling of tension.

Materials: Pussy Willow, Bertram Anderson, and Rudbeckia
Vase: Alessi, Zaha Hadid design

Materials: Peony and Pokeweed
Vase: Susumu Zaima

Simplicity often leads us to consider the deeper meaning of an arrangement. "Beauty can be better appreciated when seen mysteriously"—the less visual information that is offered, the more space is opened for personal storytelling. It's an opportunity not only to capture the beauty of the flowers themselves, but to also invite viewers to look at things in a new way

As you can see in this photo, the left side of the vase is negative space. This reduces visual stress and makes the arrangement more interesting.

Flowers and plants look more alive with more space, and each material is able to be its best. It's a more thoughtful and friendly arrangement than packing floral materials into a limited space.

It is often said that Ikebana is about arranging space or space design. Therefore, you need to practice not only arranging floral material, but also arranging the space. As you look at the other arrangements in this book, note how the space is used.

Color Theory

Colors influence our lives from the very beginning. They can attract or distract attention, set a mood, and even affect our emotions and perceptions.

Arranging flowers is also arranging colors. Colors are the first impression of the arrangement. In addition to design, color combinations can also make an impact.

Before creating a floral arrangement, you need to select your flower materials. If you are pleased with your selection, then I would say that half of your arrangement has already been successful! If you pay attention to the color combination, your arrangement will be even more amazing. Just as you color-coordinate the clothes you wear each day, choosing the right color combination of flowers is equally important. So enjoy choosing a colorful floral mix.

I get my inspiration for floral arrangements from many sources, fashion being one. I draw inspiration from fashion photos in magazines and Instagram. The color coordination in fashion photos always enthralls me. They are so chic! I save my favorite pictures on my iPhone to reference later.

Hue Circle

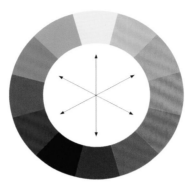

Hue Circle: A circular diagram in which "hues" of colors are listed

As I touched on earlier in the **Creation Tips: Mass, Line, Color** section, a hue circle (also called color wheel or color circle) is a chart of colors arranged in a circle as a method for systematically organizing colors. This helps me to check which color combinations will create the most impact as contrasting colors or complementary colors. I can look at the wheel to help me visualize color combinations that go well together.

Flowers with colors that are on opposite sides of the color wheel will provide a high-contrast and high-impact color combination—together, these colors will appear brighter and more prominent.

Two colors that are side by side on the color wheel will provide a subtle and conservative color combination. Florals with complementary colors bring harmony.

Keep these principles in mind when choosing which colors to use in your arrangements.

Color Combination
Tutorials

Lily and Pandanus
Vase: Stone Pot

This arrangement uses the contrasting colors of red and green. They are on opposite sides of the color wheel and are the maximum color combination impact for each other. Most of the foliage is green, so the red flower is always a brilliant queen in any arrangement.

Use your fingers to gently curve the pandanus. Point one to the right, the other to the left. Then, insert them into the kenzan.

Place one stem of lily peeking out from behind the pandanus.

Cover the kenzan with pebbles so it doesn't show.

Lily, Pandanus, and
Song of India
Vase: Antique White Porcelain Vase

As in the previous arrangement, red and green are used for maximum color drama. A kenzan is placed on the bottom of the vase. All materials are inserted on the vase's left side to create negative space. The way the pandanus is folded at a sharp angle and arranged facing downward also adds to the arrangement's strong impact.

Spray Rose and Cornflower

Vase: Rosenthal

This arrangement has a beautiful contrast of
yellow and blue flowers. Soft and windswept,
both flowers are about the same small size,
creating a gentle and delicate harmony.

The key to easily putting together an
arrangement with many lines is to create a focal
point. In this arrangement, the focal point is a
mass of six flowers facing forward.

Use "mass" and "lines" to create simple yet
dramatic arrangements.

Trachelium and Craspedia

Vase: Royal Copenhagen

Delicate and intricate, trachelium stuns with
its dense cushions of purple blooms, adding a
chic, lace-like appeal to floral arrangements.
On the other hand, craspedia is sculptural yet
whimsical—something of a botanical lollipop.
Stems of craspedia can punctuate arrangements
with pops of yellow.

Neither have petals and are not particularly
glamorous, but by combining them, they create
a unique arrangement that makes the best use of
each other's colors. To create this arrangement,
begin by placing a kenzan at the bottom
of the vase.

First, add stems of trachelium until the lines
are pleasing. Then, add the yellow color of
craspedia. Don't forget to place some stems in
the back of the arrangement to create depth.

Similar Color Combination Tutorials

Another way to play with colors is by using similar colors in combination as opposed to using contrasting colors. Using similar colors will make your arrangement restful to the mind and pleasing to the eye. This method will also give your arrangement a sense of unity, but be careful not to make it monotonous.

Ammi Visnaga, Snow-on-the-Mountain, Lisianthus, and Palm Leaf
Vase: Wedgewood

This arrangement is a combination of greens with a hint of white accents. Each of the three floral materials used in this arrangement contain both colors! The naturalistic palette of rich green and the white vase keeps the overall composition harmonious.

For this kind of upright style, place the tallest floral material into the kenzan first in order to create a framework and visualize the next step. Then, add the others in a way that you find visually pleasing. Place the palm leaf last as a sharp accent.

Oriental Bittersweet, Rudbeckia, and Ruscus
Vase: Glazed Pottery Vase

This arrangement looks stunning, especially during fall, using yellow and brown colors in a rustic brown vase. The colors of the flowers and the vase are matched to create harmony.

The gentle flowing curve created on the right side adds beautiful movement. The single standing branch and green leaves are well-balanced connections between the left and right sides of the arrangement.

Placing the flowers upward gives the overall form a lively look.

Chamomile, Spray Rose, and Curly Willow

Vase: Wedgewood

Using the same color flowers creates harmony much more effectively than using different colors.

In this arrangement, the yellow in the small disc of chamomile and the miniature blooms of spray rose are matched. I like to subtly match colors in this way to give arrangements understated refinement.

By arranging the spray roses vertically and placing the curly willow branches in an upright position, the arrangement is sleek and sophisticated.

Lily, Red Pepper, Alstroemeria, and Trachelium

Vase: Rosenthal

Similar color combinations give the look of a well-organized arrangement. This arrangement would look very different if the flowers were contrasting in color.

I hadn't thought of this flower combination, but I stumbled upon it by accident as they were lined up next to each other in the corner of my kitchen where I keep all my flowers.

I took great pleasure in making this arrangement because it was the perfect combination of flowers for this tutorial.

Color Gradiation Tutorials

Creating Ikebana using various shades of the same color can be exceptionally beautiful. Here are several arrangements for you to do to hone your skills. The idea is to replicate the hues and gradient tones found in nature. So delicate, expressive, and mysterious when observed closely, the color gradients are deeply visually engaging.

Ranunculus and Italian Ruscus
Vase: Venini

Often referred to as the rose of the spring, ranunculus is one of the most popular cut flowers. Their rose-like blooms have tissue-thin petals and they come in colors that range from cream and pale yellow to apricot, pink, orange, red, and burgundy.

In this arrangement, I blend their rich color variations together to create a beautiful gradation. Peach, apricot, orange, and pear colors...what a variety of delicious-looking hues!

The roundness of the vase is also arranged to connect with the flow of ranunculus. The pale blue of the Venetian glass is a good contrasting color for the orange ranunculus here, creating an overall harmony.

Delphinium, Cornflower and Curly Willow
Vase: Wedgwood

These blue flowers are reminiscent of the colors of the sky and sea. Blue cornflowers and pale blue delphinium create a beautiful gradation.

Most often grown for its dramatic tall spires of blue blooms, elegant delphinium adds a strong vertical element, so I created an upright style for this arrangement.

Carefully observe the color of delphinium and choose some stems that have nice color gradation. Insert four or five stems of delphinium into the kenzan to create a gently semi-spiral upright style. Keep the front stem short and place the long stems in order going up to the right, with the back stem being the longest. To balance this semi-spiral on the right side, add one stem of delphinium on the left side.

Next, insert some blue cornflowers into the kenzan to add additional color gradation.

Finally, position some curly willow on the left side of the arrangement for visual balance.

Keep the arrangement neat by bringing the bottoms of the stems together in one mass.

Because the vase is white, I use a white cloth to hide the kenzan. Pebbles can be substituted if you prefer.

You can see the difference in the arrangement's elegance when you cover the kenzan.

As kenzans age, their colors darken, so try not to show them when using a white or light-colored vase.

Pastel Color Combination Tutorials

Like airy meringues, pastel color combinations look sweet and delicious. Using pastels is a lovely way to create a soft atmosphere in Ikebana arrangements. Pastel colors are also compatible and light enough to allow multiple color combinations in one arrangement. One of the nice things about pastels is that you do not have to settle on just one color in the design. The same isn't always true for deeper jewel tones or brighter hues.

With pastels, note that the form and shape of floral materials are important to add dramatic variation to your arrangement. Because pastel colors are less bright and saturated, they are often associated with calming and peaceful vibes. Their soft look is soothing and easy on the eyes. Color can change the look of your arrangement, and it's even known to impact the viewer's mood. So let's play with colors and hone your color combination skills.

Calla, Ranunculus, and Astilbe
Vase: Stone Pot

This is a simple upright style. Milk and honey-like ranunculus, gently curved and silky purple calla, and feathery astilbe plumes create dramatic vertical composition. The colors are soothing, so the arrangement creates a soothing aesthetic.

It is important to place flowers at the back of the arrangement to create depth for a complex design. Be sure to cover the kenzan with pebbles.

Golden Rain Tree, Chrysanthemum, and White Sage
Vase: Wedgwood

Golden rain tree has cute tiny flowers on each of its branches, so I use the pastel yellow of chrysanthemum to match them. This pastel color arrangement is feminine and soft.

Place a bunch of the golden rain trees on the left side of the vase, draping down toward the table. Next, add in some chrysanthemum stems on the right side of the vase. This will create mass along with the golden rain trees that were put in earlier.

To finish up, position white sage and extra golden rain trees to gracefully dance as lines.

Because the vase has shoulders, this arrangement doesn't need any fixture or a kenzan to support the botanicals.

Neutral Colors Combination Tutorials

You may be wondering what neutral colors are like in Ikebana arrangements. I've arranged all kinds of color palettes, but when I get tired of creating colorful arrangements, I use neutral color combinations for a change.

This is also an opportunity to use dried flowers because many flowers that used to be bright eventually fade to a beige or brown hue. Neutral colors are far from boring—they're calming, soft, quiet, fresh, and very much in style. With a refined palette of neutrals, qualities like texture, form, and shape become even more important.

Texture, especially, is a way to add variation to a neutral palette. Mixing different textures of flowers or plants (e.g., smooth, rough, shiny, fluffy, shaggy, fuzzy, spiky) will keep the arrangement pulled together and interesting at the same time.

This is a fun and quiet play of color tones when arranging flowers.

Ilex Winter Gold, Rose, and Spray Rose
Vase: Marloe Marloe

Muted colors of ilex winter gold and roses can be beautifully arranged together. The overall movement is bold, but the mood is quiet.

The branch is bent into a lovely curve and placed on the left side of the vase.

I used two different rose sizes to add movement to the arrangement. Note that you will need to use a kenzan to stabilize the floral materials

Amaranthus Hot Biscuits, Ranunculus, Calla, and Curly Willow

Vase: tomoro pottery

This arrangement coordinates the beige colors of the floral materials and the vase. The tones of amaranth, ranunculus, and curly willow fit well with the color of the vase bottom. The rich textures of the fluffy amaranth, the wavy curly willows, and the ranunculus with many layers of thin petals create an expressive movement within the calm, peaceful tones. Calla lily, the straight line of pale green that breaks through the beige diversity, adds a fresh accent.

Carnation and Solidago

The exquisite colors of the withering flowers are so attractive, I can't help but arrange them. Even after colors have faded, they are still to be appreciated.

Here, both carnations and solidago have passed their best time of blooming, but when they are combined together within the same color tone, their new beauty is revealed.

Dusty Colors Combination Tutorials

Dusty color combinations are some of my very favorite color schemes.

I was at the local flower market looking around at all the different flowers when I found this dusty pink carnation. I was immediately inspired to create Ikebana using this color.

It was a wonderful find because I am always looking for something inspirational with the potential to be part of a lovely, unexpected arrangement.

Carnation, Globe Thistle, Variegated Lily Grass, and White Sage
Vase: Marloe Marloe

In addition to the color combination, the curved lines of lily grass make this arrangement especially dramatic.

First, you need to insert three stems of carnations into the kenzan, and then position white sage and globe thistle.

Next, add the graceful lines of the lily grass to bring the arrangement to life.

As your Ikebana skills grow, you will become adept at reshaping botanicals to fit a design.

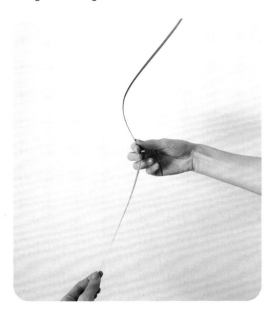

Most plant leaves can be shaped gently. To add a graceful curve to the lily grass, gently rub and stretch it with your fingers until you get the desired curve.

Creating Botanical Sculpture

"Imagination is more important than knowledge. For knowledge is limited to all we know and understand, while imagination embraces the entire world, and all there ever will be to know and understand."
—Albert Einstein

Once you have mastered Ikebana's techniques, lean into your imagination. This method works well for me, so I hope it will help you too.

Picture this: your flowers are posing in front of your camera like models, or moving like dancers. Imagine you are a movie director, a photographer, a conductor, or an interior designer. One of my Ikebana friends told me that flowers are like music for her. She loves rock music, and her floral arrangements have bright rhythms. It is your job to get the best final image using whatever creative process works best for you.

I start by visualizing an arrangement in my mind. Even if I can't see how I should complete the arrangement, I have some idea of how to begin. I think of my flowers as dancers, with stems like long necks, long arms, and long legs. It's probably because I studied ballet when I was a little girl. My body still remembers the ballet movements. When I am in the creative zone, I feel like I am the flowers' choreographer, and the arrangement is our dance. I also use this method in the **Single Botanical Ikebana** chapter on page 143.

Before you create an arrangement, think about what your flowers symbolize and create a sculpture-like arrangement. What stimulates your senses? Your flowers will reflect that. In other words, Ikebana is a reflection of you. When I enjoy other people's Ikebana arrangements, I am not only appreciating their design, I am also imagining what kind of person arranged it. Ikebana arrangements are an extension of the creator's inner self.

My Ikebana teacher, Kaz Yokou Kitajima, taught me the phrase, "If you talk to the flowers, they will always respond to you." This is a truth I cherish.

Use your imagination to find your own Ikebana style.

Sculptural Style Tutorials

Ranunculus
Vase: Ryota Aoki

This sculpture-like arrangement uses only ranunculus, which have delicate, hollow stems. Most of the stems are straight, but some are curved or bent. I used those quirky stems to create "mass" and "line" compositions. A black kenzan is used to match the black vase.

Observe your floral materials carefully and look for interesting curves and lines that can add a sense of sculpture to your Ikebana. Let your imagination soar.

Carnation, Globe Thistle, Variegated Lily Grass, and White Sage

I was playing with lily grass to get an inspiration for a next arrangement. I bundled them together, twisting, bending, and weaving, trying to find the perfect silhouette. When I placed the bundled lily grass vertically into a kenzan, I added some beautiful curves and was surprised by the outcome—the lily grass turned out to be an abstract sculpture!

I positioned one stem of carnation to support the bundled lily grass, wrapping the leaf tips around the stems of the carnation. The carnation looks like a head, and the abstract object turns into a statue.

To complete the arrangement, I added planet-like globe thistles to this alien-like statue.

You can see the leaf tips wrapped around the stems of the carnation.

Viewers can enjoy the eccentric movement of the lines.

The lily grass is tied with a rubber band and placed into the kenzan.

Variegated Lily Grass, Chrysanthemum, and Solidago

This is another version of the lily grass sculpture with different ingredients. Just one stem of chrysanthemum and solidago are added on the bottom of the left side. Their colors match the green tone, creating a feminine aspect.

Dahlia and Aspidistra
Vase: Susumu Zaima

The main feature of this arrangement
is the contemporary silhouette of the
aspidistra leaves.

First, cut a little slice in the middle of the
aspidistra leaf and insert the leaf top through
the slice. Next, bend the tip of the leaf
further, or pass it through the cut middle of
another aspidistra so that the aspidistra are
joined to make a single object.

Aspidistra is very commonly used in Ikebana
arrangements. Use your imagination and
create different shapes. Take your time
to experiment.

Remember that once you finish your creation,
you should step back and objectively
observe it from a short distance and then
make fine adjustments as needed.

Coreopsis, Marigold, and Pandanus

Here is another arrangement featuring the sculpture-like silhouette of leaves. The vivid color contrast of green and orange creates visual impact.

To create the base of this arrangement, shape the pandanus leaves by bending, weaving, twisting, and curving them, and then insert them into a kenzan. Pandanus leaves have good hardness and are easy to shape, so you can be creative with how you adjust them.

Next, to add a little bit of brightness, place coreopsis and marigold between the leaves.

The eccentric shape of the leaves can be enjoyed from any angle. In Ikebana, the arrangement is actually not only viewed from the front but also viewed from at least 180 degrees if there is a wall, or even 360 degrees if the arrangement is a centerpiece. As your Ikebana skills improve, it is important to consider each viewer's standpoint.

Delphinium and Paperplant (Fatsia Japonica)
Vase: Astier de Villatte

I keep most of my flowers in a corner of my kitchen before arranging them. One day I noticed some delphinium randomly arranged in a temporary vase, similar to this composition. Something about the way the flowers interacted inspired me.

I decided to recreate the composition intentionally. As I arranged it, it started to look like a ballet dancer posing. Don't the paperplants look like a green tutu? You can always try to capture such a perfect moment by being sensitive to the surroundings of the flowers.

Since the mouth of the vase is narrow, no fixture was needed for this composition.

To create it yourself, place a few stems of delphinium together in the vase, allowing them to support each other for stabilization.

Next, adjust the lengths and angles to recreate the composition.

To finish, place two stems of paperplants at the bottom.

A corner of my kitchen. I often get inspiration from where flowers and greenery are randomly lined up.

Stock, Variegated Aspidistra, and Lemon Leaf
Vase: Wedgwood

White and green arrangements are very popular regardless of trends. For this arrangement, I selected variegated aspidistra leaves, which have dramatic and bold white and green stripes; each leaf shows a different pattern. I used these striped patterns effectively, creating a beautifully curved flow that extends upward.

Next, place white stock flowers vertically at different heights.

The lemon leaf added at the end is also placed along the upward lines of the overall flow.

Part Two:

Ikebana Arrangements

The Single Botanical Ikebana

In this lesson, you will learn the technique of making *freestyle* arrangements. Freestyle Ikebana is divided into two types: arrangements that are naturalistic and those that are abstract and emphasize design rather than nature. You can create either in this lesson. The main difference is the materials you choose.

It is a more stylistic technique that may take some practice but it is a good place to begin (even if your first attempts do not turn out as you would like them to) because it requires practice of some of the fundamental techniques of Ikebana. I took an entire series of basic classes before I could successfully create freestyle arrangements. But once I mastered the technique, I became even more obsessed with creating thoughtful flower arrangements with fewer elements.

In the basics section, you learned that three lines are required to create a three-dimensional space. That concept has to become deeply ingrained, so it's important to practice the basic techniques. When I first learned Ikebana, I wondered why I had to repeat this method over and over again, but now I understand. By using three different lines, a space with effective movement is created. After I mastered that concept, I was able to make multiple dimensions as well.

I learned to observe materials and then work with them. Everything begins with looking at the material carefully: lines, angles, shapes, sizes, and textures should all be considered.

In this lesson, you will learn to create beautiful, simple arrangements using a single material—for example, all one kind of flower. Arrangements with only one flower variety can be boring if they are simply put into a vase in a bunch. But if you use Ikebana techniques, your arrangement will be lively and lovely. Here's how:

Using the same material gives a sense of unity. The next step is to add flow and movement to it. Because you will be working with only type of flower, the key is to be intentional about placement. Each flower should be perfectly set into the kenzan/frog or vase, with the bud facing in a direction that is pleasing to the eye. As you arrange the flowers, do so studiously, without hesitation or waste The intentional movement of the body is important to the art form.

I often make this kind of arrangement at home. Most of the flower stores around me sell flowers in bunches, which requires me to buy five to ten stems of the same type of flower. In Santa Monica where I live, the closest flower shops are grocery stores and farmers' markets. I don't want to buy too many flowers and waste any of them, so I created this single-material method because minimal waste is important to me. It makes me feel good to use everything I bring home.

Interestingly, most flower shops in Japan sell flowers by the stem, so people can choose how many stems they want in any combination.

Visualize the composition before you begin arranging and as you place stems. Once you begin, relax, and feel the flow and movement of the flowers and your body as you place them. The more you practice, the more your composition skills will improve.

Create Your Work Space

- Begin by selecting a vessel for your arrangement and fill it with water.
- Choose your cutting tool, which is scissors for stems or a small saw for branches.
- If you have chosen a shallow vase or bowl, place a kenzan at the bottom.
- Gather your flowers, foliage, or branches and place them in a vase of water to keep them hydrated until it is time for the stems to be cut and placed.
- Observe the flowers carefully to find their character, especially their face orientations and stem lines.

Because creating Ikebana with a single botanical is the best way to get started, I have included several examples here for you to try.

Anemone
Vase: Vintage Silver Bowl

Anemones have cute black or green button centers and frilly petal collars. Anemone arrangements are usually domed-shape like a bouquet, or expansive and airy, using their bendy stems. But with Ikebana techniques, you can bring out the unique beauty of anemone.

For this look, just five stems of anemone are inserted into a kenzan at different lengths and in different directions to create a stylish, poetic arrangement. At least one flower should face forward to create a focal point, which is the lowest anemone in this arrangement. This arrangement utilizes anemones alone.

> It is very important to organize the bottom of the stems neatly, otherwise the arrangement will look dull.

Poppy
Vase: Wedgewood

With their tissue paper petals and skinny, tendril-like stems, poppies are so ethereal that they seem to practically float on air.

Vary the stems' heights and directions. At least one flower should face forward to create the focal point of the arrangement. If the stems are too thin to be inserted into the kenzan, wrap paper around them or use thicker stems to reinforce them.

Calla Lily

Vase: Marble Stone Vase

This arrangement is based on the image of
a flower popping out of a vase with energy.
Gradually change the angle to create
gradation. The face of the tallest calla lily is
inserted upward to add momentum. If the face
of this flower is facing downward, the entire
arrangement will be flat. The various directions
that the calla lily leaves face add a sense of
dynamism to the arrangement.

Strawflower

Vase: Marloe Marloe

Strawflowers can be arranged fresh and appreciated as everlasting still life once dried. Their foliage browns quickly, so remove the leaves before arranging.

Place the strawflowers into a kenzan, cutting the stems to different heights so that there is a low cluster on the right side of the vase. Change the directions and angles of the flowers in various ways to add movement to the arrangement.

Remember that short arrangements can be seen from above, so it is important that they look beautiful from all angles.

This can easily become a multi-botanical Ikebana if you combine the blooms with other greenery. I added a few eucalyptus branches because both strawflowers and eucalyptus dry out beautifully, so the arrangement will be long-lasting.

The Minimalist Arrangement

It sounds simple, but it is surprisingly difficult to create minimalist arrangements that are serene and beautiful.

When I was learning Ikebana, I only worked on creating them once or twice a month. I thought that would be enough for my skill to improve, but it didn't. It was not enough for me at all, so I recommend that you practice more frequently than I did at first. Once I spent more time on the art, I got better. I perfected my Ikebana techniques and honed my skills. Just as they say, "practice makes perfect."

Botanicals bring nature inside the home. Being around flowers really does make us feel wonderful. In this lesson, I will show you a minimalist freestyle arrangement using a variety of materials.

As I noted in **The Single Botanical** lesson, freestyle does not use any special form. It will be your own style and can be vertical or horizontal. A tip for this arrangement is to combine mass and lines, creating multi-dimensional space. Be sure to add flow by connecting mass and lines (for a refresher on "mass" and "line," see page 14). A mass alone, or lines alone, is a little bland, so it is best to combine them. Moreover, when you add color combinations, it will make your arrangement even more engaging.

If you get confused and lost while designing, there are two ways to fix an arrangement that isn't coming together the way you expected it to. The first is to look at your arrangement from a distance. It allows you to see it objectively and then observe what needs to be changed. The second is to take away materials one by one until you are satisfied with the results, and then, if you want to start adding material back in, you can redesign your arrangement.

Also, remember that Ikebana is both physical and emotional. Try to arrange the flowers quickly, before you have a chance to overthink the placement. This process technique is truly helpful—when I think about the perfect placement too much, my arrangement usually ends up with unsatisfying results. The best, most advanced Ikebana arrangers I've watched are very quick to make their arrangements. So don't overthink things, and know that you will become more decisive as your skill grows.

Because this lesson features a minimalist arrangement, choose either florals, branches, or foliage that are similar in color so they work in simple harmony.

If you would like to create a large, dramatic arrangement, choose a large vessel. No matter the size, this minimalist style is simple to create, but note that a large arrangement may require more support.

Create Your Work Space

- Select a vessel for your arrangement and fill it with water.
- If using a shallow or wide vessel, place your kenzan at the bottom.
- Place your scissors where they are easily available.
- Gather flowers, foliage, or branches and place them in a vase of water to keep them hydrated until it is time for the stems to be cut and placed.
- Observe each element carefully to find the most beautiful angle of flower, leaf, or branch.

Poppy and Italian Ruscus
Vase: Astier de Villatte

Single botanical arrangements can also work well to create a minimalist style. This arrangement uses a horizontal style with greenery. Since poppy petals are so thin and fragile, in this style, the blooms show us a new side of their beauty. In an upright style, flowers look very bright and cheerful; arranging the flowers horizontally shows the sorrowful side of their beauty. I created this arrangement to express the poppies' pursuit of light.

Calla Lily
Vase: Marloe Marloe

Three stems of calla lily and their leaves are placed into a kenzan. Because the stems of calla lily are very soft, you can make them straight or bent. In this arrangement, the tallest calla lily was gently bent. The second tallest one retains the natural curve.

The calla lily leaves are disassembled from the flower stems and reassembled into an ideal position. Showing the leaves' back side adds a modern feeling to the overall arrangement.

Oriental Bittersweet

Vase: Susumu Zaima

One thing to remember is that the quality of a
flower depends on the vase. The simpler the
arrangement, the more important the quality of
the vase. A fine vase enhances the minimalist
beauty of the flower.

This arrangement is created with such a sense
of inevitability that nothing more could be
added or subtracted. It is as if the oriental
bittersweet is growing on rocks in nature.

To recreate this arrangement, separate the leaves from the flower stems and use individual leaves and stems one by one. The leaves themselves are elegant and an important element of the arrangement.

Lily of the Valley
Vase: Tobe Ware Vase

I unexpectedly found some lily of the valley, with sweetly scented bell-shaped white flowers, at the market and thought they would be perfect for a minimalist style arrangement.

With the Japanese *tokonoma* (alcove where items for artistic appreciation are displayed) in mind, I set up a square vessel and placed the arrangement in it.

A black kenzan is invisible in the black vase, so there is no need to hide the kenzan. It allows you to express the beauty of the flowers themselves as they are.

Lavender and Eucalyptus Silver Bells

Vase: Yui Tsujimura

Most often, I choose flowers for my arrangement first and then choose a vase to go with them. For this arrangement, I was inspired by this vase and then matched the botanicals to go with it.

I wanted to create something that tugs on the heartstrings without fancy flourishes and colors. so I created a vertical-style arrangement in a refined and playful way with a subdued, minimalist color tone.

The trick is to place one long lavender stem standing up straight to bring a sense of dignity to the arrangement.

Eucalyptus silver bells are secured by intertwining the branches without using wire. To create depth, put the floral materials not only on the front side of the vase, but also on the vase's back side in a well-balanced composition.

It's a uniquely shaped vase, so I made a special fixture for it by bending the flexible curly willows into arch shapes and placing two in the vase to make a cross fixture

Japanese people are very familiar with chrysanthemum flowers. In fact, in Japan there is a festival known as *Choyo*, or the Chrysanthemum Festival, which is celebrated by decorating with chrysanthemum flowers and drinking chrysanthemum sake with chrysanthemum petals floating on it in hopes of having a long life. It is one of the five sacred ancient festivals, usually celebrated on September 9.

Wild chrysanthemums are dainty, gentle, and dignified—perfect for minimalist arrangements.

To create a deep, well-balanced composition, put the floral materials both on the front and back sides of the vase.

Flowering Quince
Vase: Susumu Zaima

Although this arrangement is an example of Ikebana in the minimalist style, it is also a "Branches Arrangement" or "Single Material Arrangement," so keep this botanical in mind for any of these three types of Ikebana. Rather than creating gorgeous arrangements with abounding flowers, I prefer to create unpretentious, beautiful arrangements with a limited number of materials in earthy vases.

In this arrangement, I simply assemble and organize the quince branches until I find a composition I like. Bend or break them and trim excess twigs if necessary to create the desired composition.

Arrange the branches boldly to create dramatic and poetic "lines" and make "mass" to counterbalance the visual weight. In this arrangement, I placed quince blooms low in the middle of the vase to create small mass.

Material: Chamomile and Ivy
Vase: Shimpei Zaima

Since this is the last arrangement of this chapter, I wanted something serene and peaceful. I feel that, now more than ever, moments to commune with the natural world and be humble have never been more important. Greatness exists in the inconspicuous and overlooked details. Things found in the minor and ephemeral are beautiful. We need to slow way down sometimes. Quiet solitude can actually bring about creativity.

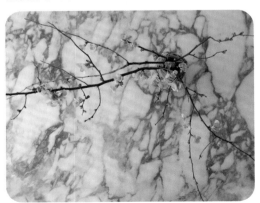

Modern Wall Flower

Wreath in Ikebana Style

Walls are not just for hanging pictures or paintings, they are also a great place to decorate with flowers. While Ikebana arrangements are lovely on tables, cabinets, and shelves, floral wall decorations brighten up any space, bringing a little patch of garden inside.

The history of wall vase arrangements in Japan is very old. In the Muromachi period (1336–1573), flowers were already used to decorate the tokonoma (alcove where art or flowers are displayed) pillar in a Japanese-style reception room.

In Japan, it is customary to decorate walls with flowers in a vase. Most wall vases are small, so they require only a few flower materials. By using flowers and foliage from your garden, you can casually incorporate the seasons into your daily life. A few simple materials artfully placed can set a mood or tell a story. Small, delicate things are often the most meaningful.

Through Ikebana, playing and working with flowers, you become a better observer of the natural world. That understanding will allow you to arrange their expressions effectively. Even your smallest arrangement will be artistic, and viewers will be deeply moved.

If the flower vase is displayed above eye level, your arrangement will be viewed from below, so the composition must take the viewer's eye level into consideration.

Wall flower arrangements also work well with dried floral materials. Not only are dried flowers beautiful, they can sometimes be reused from Ikebana made with fresh flowers if they have dried beautifully. I don't like wasting flower materials, so I keep a lot of dried flowers and branches in my house.

Making large wall arrangements is so easy and fun, and the video of me making one with my son was a hit on Instagram!

Unlike ordinary Ikebana works, wall arrangements do not have a specific compositional starting point. The purpose of this project is to expand the range of your expression, so please try to work with completely different and free-flowing ideas.

Ikebana techniques can be used to create easy and festive wreaths. Every holiday season, I hold a wreath workshop. My wreath workshop is open to anyone who is curious about arrangements, so it is fun for people of all experience levels. Just as in Ikebana, we use mass and line techniques for making wreaths. I think an Ikebana wreath is something unexpected and unusual. It is the kind of decorative piece that will surprise people. For a party, you could lay your wreath flat on the table, perhaps even with a candle, to create a stunning seasonal centerpiece. If you would like to try a new wreath style, this is it.

Create Your Work Space

- Select a vessel for your arrangement and fill it with water.
- Place your scissors where they are easily available.
- Gather flowers, foliage, or branches and place them in a vase of water to keep them hydrated until it is time for the stems to be cut and placed.
- Observe each element carefully to find the most beautiful angle of flower, leaf, or branch.

Pandorea Vine and Philadelphus

Vase: Kohchosai Kosuga Bamboo Vase

The good thing about wall vases is that you can let the vine grow toward the floor. The highlight of the wall vase arrangement is its light, airy appearance, so using a lot of floral materials is not suitable in this case. To make your arrangement come alive, it is very important to place the materials facing forward.

To show the flowing line, gently bend the vine into a wide loop on the left side. You can add any seasonal flowers, foliage, vines, and fruits, just as you might encounter them in the garden. Do be careful not to make an arrangement that is too heavy to be hung!

To place the philadelphus facing forward, break the stem so that you can create the angle you want. The break is made so that the stem can brace itself against the inner wall of the vase.

Try using Ikebana techniques to create an arrangement with depth. Dimensional arrangements are so beautiful, even when viewed from the side.

Craspedia, Safflower, and Pittosporum

Vase: Yui Tsujimura

This arrangement looks like floating yellow berries coming out of the vase. Even with a small vase, you can create a beautiful composition by creating "mass" and "line," to create a smooth flow. Don't add too many elements—keep it simple.

This is a different version of the previous arrangement. I added a small white chrysanthemum, but the vase might have been overwhelmed if the chrysanthemum was facing forward, so I turned it sideways and covered it up with a bit of foliage.

Most wall vases can be converted to regular vases, too.

Blue Ice Cypress, Quince Twig, and Myrtle

In this arrangement, to emphasize the beautiful texture of the vase, the twigs of flowering quince are added to create delicate movement.

This is the version placed on the table. The silver-green color of blue ice cypress matches the color of the vase very well.

The twigs and greenery are placed diagonally, not parallel, to avoid making the arrangement look uninspired. It's a small change, but it makes a big difference.

A Scene in Early Summer

The wall vase arrangement is ideal for adding an accent of rustic charm to your home. Small Ikebana is very pleasing and easy to incorporate into your daily life.

Sunflower, Gomphrena, and Barley

Vase: Kohchosai Kosuga Bamboo Vase

A small glass vase is placed inside the bamboo basket to hold floral materials. It is more fun to choose floral materials according to the season. Arrange them lightly so that it does not look heavy.

A Scene in Winter

Wall vase arrangements can be displayed anywhere, even with few flowers. They are eye-catching and great for daily life. The vase's position at the viewer's eye level (or slightly higher) is the ideal height.

Viburnum Berry and Explosion Grass

Vase: Kohchosai Kosuga Bamboo Vase

The explosion grasses are arranged upward, against the viburnum berries hanging downward. To make a beautiful connection between them, flow the long, thin leaves of the explosion grass to the left. The dense foliage of the viburnum berry becomes a good "mass" and provides a sense of stability in the overall arrangement.

Monstera, Snowberry, Celosia, Kiwi Vine, and Ruscus

Vase: Hender Scheme

This bold, unique arrangement creates an eccentric look.

First, I placed the monstera, the focal point of this arrangement. Then I added white snowberry and yellow celosia, using two different textures to create a sense of movement.

The snowberry on the upper right and the kiwi vine on the lower left are arranged to look like they are creating one long line.

Finally, carefully examine the angle and place the long kiwi vine to connect to the snowberry.

Ruscus leaf is inserted on the back side for better balance.

This is how the kiwi vine is fixed in place. I tucked it into the leather straps that are the decoration of the vase.

Rose and Viburnum Berry

Some wall vases can easily be made into hanging vases, so we have more places to display flowers.

I found a rare beige rose, so I arranged it in a hanging vase wrapped with beige leather strings and displayed it with the beige interior. Fresh green leaves of viburnum berry were added as a bright accent in the beige and white interior.

Most photos of Ikebana show the arrangements themselves, but it is also important to consider the harmony of the arrangement with its surroundings and interiors. The impression can be surprisingly different depending on where you place the Ikebana arrangement.

Dried Pussy Willow and Dried Craspedia

Vase: Yoka Good Things

These two wall vases are my favorites; their earthy and rough textures have a warm beauty. They can be displayed as wall objects without adding anything!

In this arrangement, I used dry floral materials, recycled from Ikebana arrangements I previously made. It is very rewarding when a flower or branch you love dries out beautifully. It provides another chance to be creative and allows you to arrange your flowers in new and different ways.

The wall objects set the scene for this abstract arrangement. No matter how few floral materials you use, creating shaped lines and accentuating height differences will tell a story.

Curly Willow, Silver Dollar Eucalyptus, Dried Tallow Berry, Ilex Berry, Dried Craspedia, and Eryngium

The wreath a person hangs on their front door during festive seasons reflects their personality. It is always homemade wreaths that catch my eye, and a homemade wreath makes a wonderful gift. People truly appreciate the time and effort you take to make something with your own hands.

Here I will show you how to create an organically unique wreath using Ikebana techniques. Creating wreaths is a good way to practice identifying and arranging beautiful lines because wreaths are simply a combination of lines.

Create a wreath ring from curly willow branches. These branches are malleable and can be bent into a round shape very easily. I love the look of squiggly tips that come off the curly willow. They have graceful curves, which are important decorations for the wreath.

For this wreath, I loop six branches once and clasp them where they overlap with wire. Leave the tips of the branches untangled, allowing them to flow.

Depending on how big you would like it to be, you may use more or less branches.

Start to weave some eucalyptus stems into the wreath. Twine the stems and leaves around the branches to secure them. The leaves make this wreath more natural and help to give it more shape.

Attach the dried tallow berry and dried pepperberry to the wreath with wire.

Place the lower parts of the stems into the wired section or between the branches, and then tie the stems to the branches with wire. After this, cut off any unnecessary stems.

Add more materials, leaving some of the branch base visible. For the ornaments, like the eryngium here, use a craft glue gun to secure them. Finally, add a bit of Spanish moss for an airy accent.

Curly Willow, Silver Dollar Eucalyptus, Dried Tallow Berry, Dried Pepperberry, Dried Eryngium, and Spanish Moss

As taught in the previous exercise, begin this wreath by creating a base of curly willow branches and then add the silver eucalyptus as noted above. At this point, weave in the tallow berry, the dried pepperberry, and the dried eryngium. Hang up the wreath before adding the Spanish moss. For this arrangement, I also added another branch of curly willow on the left side to create a gracefully rhythmic line, and then trimmed the overlapping leaves to expose the lines and movement of each material clearly.

The lines create considerable depth, and make this wreath enjoyable even when viewed from the side. After weeks, when the curly willow and eucalyptus dry out, the arrangement will have a more withered and rustic look.

Bottle Tree Bark, Blue Ice Cypress, and Strawflower

This is a sustainable decoration made of dried floral materials recycled from other Ikebana arrangements. The dried bark of the bottle tree is flexible and shaped into a light and organic look. Blue ice cypress is placed on the container-like spot, and a strawflower is tied at the tail-like vine, creating an enjoyable rhythm and smooth flow.

The technique of arranging lines is one of the key characteristics of Ikebana. Find the beautiful moment while experimenting with various line combinations. Using recycled materials is so meaningful to me.

Bottle Tree Bark, Hydrangea and Chinese Lantern Plant

Dried hydrangea and Chinese lantern plants are more subdued in color than when they were fresh flowers. They match to the light color of the bark and create nuance.

To dry the hydrangeas, place them in a water-filled vase, but don't top up the water; just let them dry out naturally. By the time the water has disappeared, you will have a bunch of dried hydrangeas, which last nearly forever. I keep a little bundle of them at home and pull them out when I am in need if something delicate and feminine for an arrangement.

The Center of Attention

Centerpieces are the perfect way to brighten up a table and create a beautiful atmosphere.

If you want to create an unconventional centerpiece, Ikebana is a great way to design something eye-catching. Even a small amount of floral material is enough to create a stunning, blooming centerpiece.

Since a centerpiece is placed in the middle of the table and viewed from a 360-degree angle, it should be arranged beautifully from all sides.

Although Ikebana makes wonderful centerpieces for all seasons, this one is especially perfect for summer because the clear vase allows the water to become one of the elements featured. This design is called a floating arrangement. The water becomes a part of the work, creating a cool impression.

Because this arrangement requires only a few materials, you can quickly and easily make a beautiful Ikebana arrangement for last minute get-togethers. Your guests will surely feel your warmth.

Unlike floral foam, a kenzan does not contaminate the water, so you can intentionally display the clear water in your design. Because this arrangement calls for lightweight flower materials, a plastic kenzan can be used.

Create Your Work Space

- Select a vessel for your arrangement and fill it with water.
- If using a shallow or wide vessel, place your kenzan at the bottom.
- Place your scissors where they are easily available.
- Gather flowers, foliage, or branches and place them in a vase of water to keep them hydrated until it is time for the stems to be cut and placed.
- Observe each element carefully to find the most beautiful angle of flower, leaf, or branch.

Oriental Bittersweet
and Clematis
Vase: Hasami Porcelain

Oriental bittersweet grows as a vine, so it's a good idea to take advantage of that feature by arranging it to crawl on a table. To maximize the beauty with less flower materials, the yellow berries are arranged with the contrasting purple color of the clematis.

Use a black kenzan (if you have one) when using a dark color vase, so that you don't have to hide the kenzan. If you only have a regular kenzan, try to cover it with the floral material or pebbles.

Combine several bittersweet branches to make a smooth flow. Secure them with the kenzan.

Add some clematis to finish up your arrangement. Diversify the lengths of the stems and the direction of the flowers to create movement.

Dahlia, Calluna, Dusty Miller, and Ruscus

Vase: Wedgewood

Place a kenzan in the middle of the vase and fill the vase with water until the kenzan is fully covered.

First, place calluna branches on both sides of the vase, one side upright and the other side long. Next add some dahlias.

Finally, position dusty miller and ruscus to create volume within the vase and hide the kenzan. At this point, add leaves low and in the middle so that the movement of the branches stands out.

Golden Rain Tree, Chrysanthemum, and White Sage

This arrangement moves like it is dancing in the wind. It reminds me of Marilyn Monroe flirtatiously posing over a subway grate, her white dress fluttering in the air.

To begin, place a kenzan in the middle of the vase and fill the vase with water until it covers the kenzan. Trim the withered and old leaves of the golden rain tree so that their beautiful curly lines and unique qualities are exposed. Next, insert them on both sides of the vase at different heights, one side taller and the other side shorter.

Trim and add the chrysanthemum low in the middle of the arrangement to create "mass" and hide the kenzan. Arranging the chrysanthemums this way gives the entire arrangement a lot of movement.

Finish by placing the white sages to connect branches and flowers, to create a graceful flow.

Because this is a centerpiece arrangement, make sure it will be beautiful from all directions.

Dahlia, Garlic Flower, Song of India, Dusty Miller, and Ruscus

Vase: Hasami Porcelain

In this arrangement, I use two kenzans in the vase: one three-inch kenzan and another smaller one. Showing the water between the two groupings is an important feature of this arrangement. The composition of the flowing water creates a tranquil and serene atmosphere.

Next insert some garlic flowers, following the same procedure as for the dahlias. Place song of India on both sides to make spiky accents, and then add dusty miller and ruscus to fill the gaps. These three kinds of leaves create expressive "mass" in this arrangement.

Place the two kenzans on both ends of the vase and fill it with water until the kenzans are covered.

Trim and add dahlias in different lengths and directions on both sides of the kenzans. At this point, don't think too much about where to place the flowers. Simply arrange the dahlias asymmetrically to create movement.

Because this is a centerpiece arrangement, be sure it looks beautiful from all directions.

Rudbeckia, Sedum Bertram Anderson, Kangaroo Paw, and Ruscus

Vase: Susumu Zaima

This is a simple arrangement using three stems of flowers and other materials, but the color nuances between flowers and the vase moves from dark brown, orange, and yellow to give a mesmerizing quality. The vivid green of the ruscus works as a nice contrast. By placing the kenzan in the corner of the vase, you can create negative space.

Three stems of rudbeckia create beautiful "mass," and the stem and bud of kangaroo paw form "lines." It will be the most beautiful composition when the arrangement is placed diagonally in the vase. When you use the space well, even a simple arrangement looks stunning.

Flat-Style Centerpieces

I will show you three different centerpieces using one kenzan in the vase. The clear water becomes a part of your arrangement, so these are perfect when you want to create a cool look. All of them are flat-style arrangements with no height, so they can be seen well from above. Therefore, it is important to be aware of the viewer's perspective when creating these.

Poppy, Cymbidium, Tweedia, and Italian Ruscus
Vase: Wedgewood

Place a kenzan in the middle of the vase, then pour water until the kenzan is fully covered. To create "mass," insert cymbidium into the kenzan and add one stem of poppy as a main accent. Next, to create "line," position the Italian ruscus on both sides of the arrangement, one side longer and the other side shorter. Lastly, to create a beautiful connection between "mass" and "line," add some tweedia.

Pandorea Vine, Scabiosa, Philadelphus, and Hungarian Lilac (Syringa Josikaea)

Vase: Large White Porcelain

Place a kenzan in the corner of the vase, then pour water until the kenzan is fully covered.

First, make random loops with pandorea vine and let them float on the water in the vase. Next, to create "mass," insert some scabiosa into the kenzan at various angles. Lastly, to create a beautiful connection between the vine and the flowers, add philadelphus to one side of the joint and add hungarian lilac on the other side.

Pandorea Vine, Hydrangea and Lisianthus

Place a kenzan in the corner of the vase, then pour water until the kenzan is fully covered.

First, make random loops with pandorea vine and let them float on the water in the vase. Next, to create "mass," insert one stem of hydrangea into the kenzan. Lastly, to create an accent-like connection between the vine and the hydrangea, add some lisianthus to one side of the joint.

Large Centerpieces

Just a few flowers and a lot of foliage are enough to create a large centerpiece. After pruning your garden, why not reuse that greenery instead of throwing it away? This is a great project if you have a garden that you can take a real mix of cuttings from to personalize your design.

Lily, Amaranth, Pandanus, Song of India, Acacia Foliage, and Myrtle Foliage
Vase: Concrete Pot

Use two or three kenzans when you create a large arrangement. For this one, I place two three-inch kenzans in the middle of the vase.

Start by creating a foliage base with myrtle. Place a bunch of acacias, allowing the tips to arc down onto the right and left sides of the vase. Acacia's fluffy foliage and arching branches work as fixtures in the vase.

Insert the stems of lily into the kenzan, allowing them to cluster on the rim. Place two stems of the song of India on the left side. To incorporate more movement, add in myrtle branches on the right side and around the lilies.

Next, to create "lines," insert two stems of long pandanus into the kenzan, making big arcs to the left and right to match the shape of the vase. These two lines are placed slightly off-center to the left.

To finish up, take three stems of long amaranth and insert them into the kenzan on the right side of the vase, letting them cascade toward the table. To balance the long amaranth and acacia branches, gently dangle the amaranth on the acacia. Last, add more water to fill the vase.

Dynamic lines of amaranth and pandanus give this arrangement an energetic and lively finish.

The Wabi-Sabi Way

"Wabi-sabi is an aesthetic appreciation of the evanescence of life."
—Leonard Koren (*Wabi-Sabi for Artists, Designers, Poets & Philosophers*)

To explain the beautiful simplicity of Ikebana, I need to mention a little about wabi-sabi. When I started this chapter, I had to do a lot of research on wabi-sabi. I am familiar with this term; I practice wabi-sabi at traditional tea ceremonies. Still, I hesitate to use this term casually. Wabi-sabi is not a style, a fashion, or a design trend. The spirit of wabi-sabi is the intrinsic beauty that can be found in the imperfect, impermanent, and incomplete. Through wabi-sabi, we can see splendor in things modest and humble. We can find quiet magnificence in the changes of nature, including in ourselves.

Wabi-sabi contains various profound aspects, values, subtleties of thought, and meaningful aesthetics, such as the sad-beautiful feeling of desolation and melancholy. Wabi-sabi is inspiring, humble, and emotive. In my own practice, I sometimes arrange flowers quietly and with great feeling. But sometimes I am blissful; I make peaceful and simple flower arrangements cheerfully and joyously.

I am influenced by this spirit and respect it. It's about using less and enjoying the things we have more of—it's about cutting through the excess to discover what is essential.

This lesson will show you how to create arrangements that utilize a "less is more" approach, a minimal use of materials for maximum results. These designs look perfectly elegant in an understated way. In simplicity, there is serenity and stillness.

Each material, flower, branch, or foliage is carefully selected for this aesthetic composition. Observe your materials and choose your favorite. I like picking a quirky stem or curved branch. When necessary, I bend or twist the branch or stem into a shape of my liking. I then remove any excess twigs, leaves, or buds to simplify the arrangement. The key to a sophisticated arrangement is organizing all the flowers and foliage intentionally.

While you are arranging, keep in mind other techniques, such as being conscious of negative space to add a dramatic effect.

If you are not sure what to do, diversify the arrangement by making one material extremely long, tall, low, or small. You can also bend or twist the materials to build remarkable character. Always follow your intuition first, and make changes later if necessary.

There is a Japanese saying, "There is fortune in leftovers." I feel so delighted when I use leftover flowers, buds, withering flowers, and dried flowers. For me, this is the true joy of Ikebana.

Camellia Wabisuke
Vase: Hagi Ware Vase

In Japan, camellia is one of the most loved flowers of the winter season. Recently, many hybrids have been created in a variety of sizes and colors.

Every leaf is balanced at various angles.

To begin create a cross-bar fixture to secure the botanicals. Camellia wabisuke, as you see in the photo, has smaller flowers than regular camellias. Wabisuke is traditionally preferred for tea ceremonies, as garden tree and cut flower, because of its quiet appearance. Actually, this camellia was given to me by my tea ceremony teacher. It was displayed in her tearoom before she gave it to me.

The leaves are divided into four parts and placed into the vase to create my preferred angles.

The long branch extending from the graceful camellia flows to the left, creating a fleeting beauty. Because of the simple composition, the way you place the leaves is very important. If all the leaves faced forward, it would look unnatural, so placing them sideways, upward, or backward is the key to this arrangement.

Oriental Bittersweet
and Butterfly Ranunculus
Vase: Susumu Zaima

The key to the beauty of this arrangement
is the combination of all the elements. Thin
and delicately curved lines are used to
express minimal beauty: simple, modest, and
ephemeral. Remember to gather their feet
together to make the overall look organized.

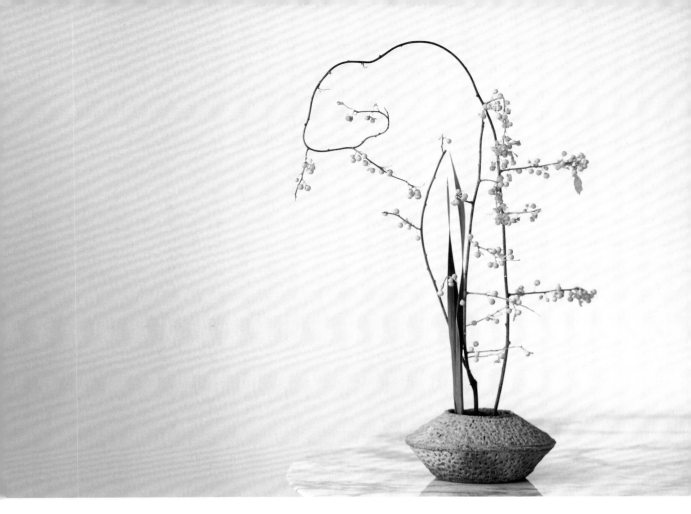

Oriental Bittersweet
and Freesia Leaves

This arrangement uses only the lines of the branches and leaves to create a subtle and evanescent expression without using flowers.

By studying the plants, you can find countless lines, including straight, curved, complicated, delicate, freely stretching, and so on. In Ikebana, one of the basic principles is to interpret the plants as lines. When you observe the lines of any plant, you can pick and choose the ones to be used in your arrangement.

Raspberry Branch, Viburnum Berry, and Lisianthus

I used sober colors to express the beauty and humility in this arrangement. According to *The Book of Tea* written by Kakuzo Okakura, the tea-masters have given emphasis to our natural love of simplicity and shown us "the beauty of humility." The book emphasizes how *Chado* (the Japanese tea ceremony) taught the Japanese many things, but most importantly, it taught them to value simplicity.

As it is written, "noisy flowers were relentlessly banished from the tea-room," so I arranged quiet flowers here.

Flowering Quince
Vase: Nelson Sepulveda Glass

Simplicity is at the core of all things wabi-sabi, and in keeping with that philosophy, this is the simplest arrangement in this book.

Originally, this branch had excessive twigs on it, so I got rid everything except for this bloom to stress the quality of the line. I used a glass vase to clearly show this single branch from foot to tip. I want it to look like the single branch is standing alone. This moment serves as a reminder of a quiet and meditative time. It is important to feel with your eyes.

Wabi-sabi is not about gorgeous flowers, not moments of bloom and lushness, but moments of inception and subsiding. Pare down to the essence, but don't remove the poetry. Every branch has its own meaning. Each viewer will interpret this artwork in a personal way. The effect of "less is more" becomes more potent, more profound. Simplicity is not so simple.

Standing Flowers

For me, one of the greatest pleasures of Ikebana is the simple pureness of beautiful flowers. Their faces are a sanctuary for the soul.

Ikebana arrangements can be created using only flowers. You don't need to prepare branches and leaves—you can complete your Ikebana with flower materials alone. Having just the essentials is better than having superfluous things. You can focus on what matters.

With sustainability being at the front of people's minds, I have tempered my use of cut flowers and focused more on simpler designs. I use many Ikebana techniques to make the arrangement look dynamic even if I am working with only leaves or branches.

You don't have to have a large variety of botanical materials to create a beautiful Ikebana. It is a very flexible method. It is used to create an unconventionally simple style of floral arrangements.

To create an Ikebana arrangement with a classic style, I may use a mass of flowers. This style looks like an art object of flowers, especially when I use larger flowers, such as peonies, dahlias, lilies, and hydrangeas. I prefer to use this classic style.

To create a more bohemian style, with an organic movement that is soft and gentle like wildflowers blooming in the field, I will place my flowers more loosely. Smaller flowers are suitable for this, such as anemones, ranunculus, tulips, calla, poppies, daisies, cosmos, sweet peas, freesia, and lisianthus. These flowers' pliant stems are suitable for this bohemian and natural style.

To organize an only-flower arrangement, you need to create mass and lines with the flowers so that your arrangement will have a clean movement. If you need a refresher on "mass" and "line," refer back to page 14.

When placing your flowers in this arrangement, keep in mind that flowers look better when they face different directions. For example, instead of a group photo where everyone is looking at the camera, try to imagine a candid scene where everyone is unaware of the camera and looking at whatever they find interesting.

You can find unique stem lines, or gently bend them to create a curve. It is charming to use features such as drooping stems, oddly shaped petals, or inconsistent sizes. The less perfect a flower is, the more character it has. Like people, this is how flowers exist naturally.

As you create arrangements in this style, feel free to be playful and try new techniques.

Create Your Work Space

- Select a vessel for your arrangement and fill it with water.
- Place your kenzan at the bottom of the vase or bowl if you are using a shallow vessel.
- Place your scissors where they are easily available.
- Gather a variety of flowers in different colors, sizes, and textures, and place them in a vase of water to keep them hydrated until it is time for the stems to be cut and placed.
- Observe each element carefully to find the most beautiful angle of flower, leaf, or branch.

Spray Chrysanthemum, White Lysimachia and Clematis
Vase: Susumu Zaima

The horizontal style, with its wide-open shape, gives the viewer a peaceful and relaxed feeling. Moreover, using only flowers (rather than a mixture of botanicals) gives this arrangement a gentle, soothing effect.

Since the mouth of the vase is small, no fixture is applied; the more you add, the sturdier the piece becomes. The spray chrysanthemum in the center of the vase forms "mass," giving the arrangement a sense of stability. The white lysimachia and the clematis form "lines," creating graceful movement.

An above-view of the arrangement

Put the flowers on the back side as well as the front to add depth.

Pincushion Protea, White Lysimachia, Veronica, and Bouvardia

Vase: White Porcelain Vase

In this arrangement, white lysimachia and Veronica are arranged to rise in the upper left direction (forty-five degrees to the left). This is the highlight of this arrangement, so the rest of the floral materials are arranged low to make the rising line stand out. The mass created in the low position gives a sense of stability to this open composition.

The two stems of orange pincushion protea accentuate the composition and colors; the longer pincushion protea is placed on the right side to contrast the rising line of the left side, and the orange color is used effectively to contrast the purple color of Veronica. Also, their leaves are removed to organize the arrangement neatly.

Sunflower, Cornflower, and Chamomile
Vase: Marloe Marloe

One of my favorite styles in Ikebana arrangement is a loose, airy, and organic style. It is not a traditional style at all. My arrangements are always changing because my Ikebana reflects my inner self. I'm very comfortable creating a natural and organic style now.

When I select floral materials, texture is important. Every single flower, foliage, or botanic has its own texture. In this arrangement, I am talking about those little, delicate, dainty textures to create this "looser" look. I found all of these floral materials at a nearby farmer's market.

First, place some cornflowers in the left side of the vase, allowing their stems to cross and

tangle to support each other and create a natural feeling, like being blown by the wind.

Cornflowers and chamomile are ideal for creating something light, airy, and dreamy. In this arrangement, they work to soften the boldness of the sunflower head.

Lastly, position the sunflower to add the arrangement's focal point.

Calla Lily and Cornflower

Vase: Astier de Villatte

This is an interesting arrangement that contrasts two types of flowers with completely different shapes, textures, and colors.

The thin, green-branched stems of cornflowers create a lacy screen, while the long, thick stem of calla lily is breaking through that lacy "mass." The overlap between the two textures creates an interesting contrast.

Two stems of calla lily are placed at the bottom of the arrangement to create a sense of stability.

Coreopsis, Marigold, Delphinium, and Lisianthus

Vase: tomoro pottery

I created a "mass" arrangement with leftover materials during Halloween time. In this arrangement, the weight is placed on the left side of the vase to create an unbalanced composition. To emphasize this impact, only the coreopsis is placed on the left side. The rest of the various flowers are added on the right side of the vase to visualize two distinct "masses."

Rather than arranging a mass of uniform material, composing masses of different colors and textures adds more variation and depth of the volume of the arrangement.

You can clearly see that the weight is placed on the left side of the arrangement.

Cosmos and Gentiana

This arrangement is similar to the Single Material Arrangements using the same botanicals, but the blue gentiana is placed low to add stability and a color accent to the arrangement.

Cosmos are quintessential cottage garden flowers, with frilly leaves and stems that are easy to arrange into an expressive look. Observe your flowers carefully to find the stems that have beautiful, curved lines and different sizes of flower heads, then insert them into a kenzan at different heights and in different directions.

Lastly, position the blue gentiana. Don't forget to organize the bottoms of the stems together to keep the arrangement tidy.

Ranunculus, Delphinium Buds, and Cornflower Buds
Vase: Simone Bodmer-Turner

This arrangement expresses the fragile beauty of withering flowers. I added delphinium buds and cornflower buds to give it more movement.

To create an organically atmospheric mood in Ikebana arrangements, rather than using natural flowers as they are, trim excess elements like leaves, twigs, and buds to organize the composition. Try not to add too many extras so you will still end up with a sophisticated look.

The Greenery Lover

This lesson features Ikebana arrangements using only green materials. When we are surrounded by greenery in a forest or field, we feel peace and healing. So for this arrangement, I want to feature the serene beauty of greenery inside.

Typically, foliage is the complement to your focal-point flowers rather than the primary element. It tends to play a supporting role, but in this lesson, it will take the lead.

Foliage comes in a variety of tones and textures, and the shapes are varied, so by combining them, you can create an unexpected and exquisite arrangement. Something like this could happily take pride of place in your interior and decorations—no flowers needed.

The beauty and versatility of green plants has a lot of potential for drama. Oversized palm leaves, monsteras, and banana leaves will add a tropical statement, while vines and lily grasses will give a graceful flow. To enrich the expression, foliage can be intertwined, rolled up, bended, etc. Even showing the back side of leaves will change the look. Moreover, these arrangements are long-lasting, easy to care for, and complement any interior, so they are a highly recommended.

Be sure to use more than two types of green plants to compose your arrangement. As I mentioned in other chapters, a tip for this arrangement is to combine mass and lines as well, so that your arrangement will have a dramatic movement.

In my Ikebana classes, I teach how to use foliage because it is equally as important as the use of flowers and branches. I tell my students over and over again that the use of foliage is key to an arrangement being refined or not. By changing the shape or angle just a little, you can change the sophistication of the entire arrangement.

Through Ikebana, I was able to discover the charm of green plants that I had previously overlooked. I hope you will discover their beauty as well.

Create Your Work Space

- Select a vessel for your arrangement and fill it with water.

- Place your kenzan at the bottom of the vase or bowl if you are using a shallow vessel.

- Place your scissors or (small saw if using branches) where they are easily available.

- Gather a variety of leaves and branches with green leaves attached, in different hues and textures. Place them in a vase of water to keep them hydrated until it is time for the stems to be cut and placed.

- Observe each element carefully to find the most beautiful angle of flower, leaf, or branch.

Palm Leaf, Monstera, and Ruscus
Vase: Bohemian Crystal Vase

In this arrangement, a mix of foliage in different shapes, sizes, and textures is combined to create a bohemian Ikebana aesthetic. The finished design looks fresh and understated—perfect for calm, peaceful spaces, or quiet areas in the home.

"Direct fixing" is applied in this arrangement. Each leaf is intertwined to create an airy and gentle atmosphere.

As an option, you can add flowers to this arrangement. In this case, I added snapdragon flowers which transforms it into a different style.

Palm Leaf, Rudbeckia, and Kangaroo Paw

Palm leaves are often used in Ikebana. Sometimes the leaves are cut off boldly, bent, sculpted, or intertwined to create a contemporary, unique composition.

In this arrangement, I cut off all the leaves on half of the palm and added a sweeping curve to the stem. Playing with palm leaves can be fun, so feel free to create your own original composition by making full use of your cutting, bending, fixing, and intertwining skills.

Monstera and Dahlia
Vase: Wedgewood

You will use "direct fixing" to create this arrangement. As you can see, monstera leaves are the main material. To create movement, choose different sizes of monstera and place them in different directions; the smaller one is upward, the larger one is downward, and one more is placed in the backside of the arrangement to create depth.

Three stems of dahlia are added peeking out from behind the monstera. A glimpse of a dahlia through the gaps of the larger monstera is poetic. The idea, metaphorically expressed, is that beauty can be better appreciated when mysterious.

One stem of the ruscus is placed to hide the empty mouth of the vase, but it is fine to leave it in view if you prefer. If it's a simple and dainty arrangement, it's unnecessary. But in this arrangement, adding the ruscus is more beautiful than without it. Don't skimp on the back of the arrangement either. Beauty is in the details.

Balloon Milkweed, Pandanus, and Myrtle

Vase: Bizen Ware

I chose three different green plants for this arrangement, each with a different shape and characteristics, to add movement and uniqueness.

Wrap the lower part of balloon milkweed with long leaves of the pandanus to create harmony in the overall arrangement.

Next, add the myrtle branch as an accent to create depth. Place on the left side of the vase to make it look like the balloon milkweed is floating in the air. That also creates negative space on the right side of the arrangement.

Two branches of the myrtle are placed at the back of the arrangement to create depth.

Make a small cut in the pandanus leaf's middle streak and slide the other pandanus through the slit. This technique of intertwining leaves is often used in Ikebana.

Lily Grass, Alstroemeria, and Snowberry

Vase: Susumu Zaima

In this arrangement, lily grasses are loosely tied together to create a graceful yet bold flow in and out of the vase. In its simplicity, this becomes a dynamic arrangement.

Alstroemeria and snowberries are added as gentle accents.

At first glance, this arrangement looks difficult, but it is surprisingly easy. First, prepare three bunches of lily grass tied with rubber bands. Next, insert them into the kenzan and tie or twine the bundles together. Any way you do it, the combination will look great.

The vase is covered with beautiful, layered lines of the lily grass. In many ways, Ikebana is the story of the relationship between nature and vases, so be aware of the harmony between the two.

Rosemary, Lily Grass, and Philodendron

Vase: Blue Glass Vase

This is a very small arrangement using leftover green plants. Even a simple, small arrangement can be delightful.

After inserting rosemary and a mini philodendron, make graceful curves with the lily grasses. Put the curved lily grasses at the front and back side to make the overall look well-balanced from any angle.

Branching Out

When the New Year begins, spring branches start to appear in the flower market. In Southern California where I live, after January first, it feels like spring comes all at once, and that brings me great joy. Although I love the flower market during the lively holiday season, I cherish that quiet, fresh moment when spring arrives.

Spring is the most exciting season for florists because so many beautiful flowers are in bloom. The most popular branches, such as quince, plum, cherry blossom, magnolia, dogwood, forsythia, lilac, spiraea, and viburnum snowball, become available in spring as well.

Because spring branches bloom with such pretty and romantic flowers, I am fond of designing arrangements with blooming branches—especially quince, cherry blossom, and magnolia branches. This allows for the most refined creations.

As spring ends and summer passes, autumn branches, such as oriental bittersweet, callicarpa (beautyberry), maple, and hypericum all arrive. As opposed to the spring branches, autumn branches are modest and austere. They create an organic and rustic feeling.

Japanese floral arrangers have always enjoyed using branches. Sculptural branches add an elegance to a space. Ikebana arrangements do not always need flowers and foliage. Branches can often be the main attraction.

Branches are a sustainable choice. They have a timeless beauty that can last for weeks, months, and sometimes semi-permanently. Finding good branches is harder than finding good flowers, so when I find stunning branches, I am super excited!

Branch arrangements implement the same techniques that have been covered in the introduction to Ikebana techniques, and now is the time to try your hand at creating an arrangement using them. Most branches have an architectural allure that creates an extraordinary composition, so observe the branches closely, find a good angle, dismantle and rebuild, and then arrange them effectively. When necessary, bend or fold the branches to create your ideal line.

Create Your Work Space

- Select a vessel for your arrangement and fill it with water.

- Place your kenzan at the bottom of the vase or bowl if you are using a shallow vessel. As a reminder, even branches can be placed in the spikey kenzan to hold them in place.

- Place your scissors, hand clippers, or small saw where they are easily available.

- Observe each branch carefully to find the most beautiful angle. If the branch is flowering, check for the side with the most blooms.

Ilex Winter Gold, Dahlia, Song of India
Vase: Green Marble Vase

This moderate Orange-yellow color is just perfect for autumn and winter. One day, when I have my own garden, I would like to plant Winter Gold.

Creating the arrangement in the horizontal style shows the full movement of the branches. I chose this dahlia because the color of the middle disc matches the winter gold berries, creating harmony.

Arrange the branches boldly to create dramatic lines and then use flowers and foliage as mass to counterbalance the visual weight.

When bending a branch, hold the point at which it is to be bent firmly with both hands. Apply pressure slowly by putting the thumbs of both hands together on this point. If you are not sure about how flexible the branch is, try it first with a spare branch you don't plan to use. Thin branches and flower stems can be bent more easily by slightly twisting.

A branch before bending is still straight. This branch is slightly flexible and easy to shape if bent carefully.

This branch was curved into a gentle bending line.

on the thickness of the branch, as well as the weight of the berries the branch must support.

Gently bend to open the cut in the branch. If you bend the branch too rapidly, it will break.

Use the same branch material to cut a small wedge and insert. The branches tend to spring back, so the wedge will be held in place.

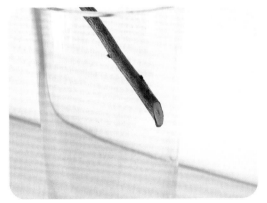

To create a sharply bent angle, cut the point of the branch at which it is to be bent at the angle you desire. How deeply you cut will depend

The ideal curve has been achieved. Bending the branches will also help them balance better in the vase. To fix the branch, cut the end of the branch diagonally so that it firmly touches the inside wall of the vase.

Once the branches are settled, add three stems of dahlia to both front and back sides. To finish up, add two stems of song of India on the left side of the arrangement.

An above-view of the arrangement. The song of India is placed a little further back to create depth.

Place three branches horizontally on both sides of the vase using a single bar fixture and stabilize the flowers and leaves for later use.

Ilex Winter Gold, Dahlia, Song of India Variation

As I did for the previous arrangement, I used a single bar fixture here as well. Position the upright branch first to decide the height of your arrangement, and then add more branches to create width.

Once the branches are settled, add three stems of dahlia on both front and back sides. To finish up, add two stems of the song of India on both sides of the arrangement.

This is a different style than the horizontal-style arrangement above, but for this I used the same floral materials.

California Pepper Tree and Dahlia
Vase: Susumu Zaima

The composition of this arrangement is very simple. It uses only one flower and one branch, but it tells the story of a beautiful dahlia sheltering from the rain under a tree. As you can see, the big curve of the pepper tree is the highlight in this arrangement.

Because this pepper tree has a big curve and it is hard to balance it in the vase even with a cross-bar fixture, I utilized a "vertical-type fixture." This method allows you to more firmly fix the branch at the desired angle if the branch to be used is thick and strong enough for splitting.

California Pepper Tree, Hydrangea, and Canterbury Bells
Vase: Pottery Bowl

Make sure that the bottom of the fixture is securely adhered to the bottom of the vase, and the split end of the branch is fixed to the vase's inner wall. When these two points stay in the vase, the branch will be firmly fixed.

To finish up, place a single dahlia upward under the pepper tree.

This is a variation of the California pepper tree arrangement. Someday, I would love to have a small garden, but for now I create this arrangement with tall trees to tide me over.

Start by trimming the excess leaves so that the clean lines of the branches can be seen. Large flowers are combined to balance with the large branches.

Remove the kenzan from the vase and place it on the table or the floor before inserting the branch so you don't accidentally crack the vase. To prevent the kenzan from scratching the table or floor, place a cloth underneath. If the branch is inserted all the way to the bottom of the needles, it will stand steady.

You will need to use a large kenzan to secure the tall, large branches of the pepper tree. Before inserting a thick branch into the kenzan, make a cut in the base of the middle of the stalk to create thinner stalks. It will make it easier to insert into the kenzan.

Curly Willow, Snowberry, Rosemary, and Ruscus

The beautifully flowing lines of curly willows look as if they are dancing with joy. To match this flow, other floral materials are arranged and create "mass" and "lines."

On the right side of curly willow, two branches of rosemary are bent sharply to add edgy accents to the flow, which is the one of the highlights in this arrangement.

The leaves of the snowberry, except for the one popping up on the right side, are trimmed because they overlap with the green of the ruscus and rosemary.

Curly willow is often used in Ikebana. Its flexibility allows it to be easily shaped, so it is a must-have item for many branch arrangements. In this section, I will show you two arrangements using curly willows as the main material. In addition to these, there are some arrangements using curly willows as an accent on other pages as well, so if you find that you love curly willow as much as I do, I have given many examples using this wonderful botanical.

Curly Willow, Eryngium, Eucalyptus Populus, and Lemon Leaf

In this unique composition, dramatic and contorted lines extend in three directions, using bunches of curly willows. An inverted S-shaped line of a thicker curly willow is placed in the middle of this arrangement to add variety.

Curly willow is very soft and flexible to shape. Bend, fold, weave, tie, and fasten with wire if necessary.

In this arrangement, the clump of curly willow is just sitting on top of the vase. But by adding stems of eryngium and foliage into the vase, the clump of curly willow will be stabilized. Plus, this clump will work as a fixture for eryngium and foliage. Make sure that the vase is full of water, to make the vase heavier and more stable.

To finish up, instead of using flowers, arrange foliage and eryngium to add a rugged texture and an organic look. At the same time, try to create "mass" with these materials to make the arrangement look well-balanced.

Cherry Blossom Branches

Cherry Blossom (or *Sakura*) is a very special tree for me, as it is for most Japanese people, because it is the national flower of Japan.

You might be surprised to know that there are more than 100 native species of cherry blossom in Japan, ranging in appearance, size, color, and timing of their bloom. In addition, there are at least 200 cultivars from these native species.

Sakura fubuki, or simply *fubuki*, means snowstorm or blizzard in Japanese, which is the state of cherry blossom falling from the sky like fat flakes of snow tumbling to the ground. The scene is fleeting and beautiful.

Here, I will show you two of the most commonly found cherry blossoms in Japan, which is *Somei Yoshino* (Yoshino Cherry Blossom) and *Yaezakura* (Double Cherry Blossom). I am very happy to have access to these cherry blossoms even though I now live in the United States.

Somei Yoshino
(Yoshino Cherry Blossom)

Somei Yoshino is the most common and iconic type of cherry blossom in Japan, with its five-petaled and white or pale pink blossoms. When we speak of cherry blossoms in Japan, this is the one that comes to mind. I simply arrange them like a little cherry blossom tree in the house for *Hanami*, which is the Japanese traditional custom of enjoying the transient beauty of flowers.

To create "direct fixing" for the previous arrangement, cross the branches to create a support for each other. The more floral material you put in the vase, the more they will be fixed in place.

To create a diagonal angle, cut the ends of the branches diagonally and touch them to the wall of the vase.

Yaezakura (Double Cherry Blossom) and Paperplant (Fatsia Japonica)

Yaezakura, which means multi-layered cherry blossom, is a catch-all term for cherry blossoms with more than five petals. *Yaezakura* have petals that range from light to dark pink. They sometimes resemble peonies, so some people also call them *botan-zakura*, as *botan* is the Japanese word for peony.

Two branches of *Yaezakura* and two stems of paperplant are used in this arrangement. Both branches are bent to create a gentle curve and crossed around the middle, so that they look like two people snuggling.

As a variation, you can also use branches of cherry blossoms alone to create an arrangement as large as a tree.

A cup of *Sakura-cha* (cherry blossom tea)

Sakura-cha, literally "cherry blossom tea," is a Japanese infusion created by steeping salt-pickled cherry blossoms in boiled water. This combination has become a type of herbal tea that has been enjoyed for many generations in Japan. This tea is served during celebrations, often at marriage ceremonies. The pink petals spreading in the hot water are so pretty.

Salt-pickled cherry blossom is often used as a topping for rice cakes and rice balls, as well as any other sweets or dishes. My friend Seiko Odashima, who is a teacher of fermentation food in Los Angeles, made homemade pickled cherry blossoms for me. She used *Yaezakura* (Double Cherry Blossom) buds for these beautiful pieces.

Tulip Magnolia
Vase: Susumu Zaima

Magnolia is one of the most beloved flowering trees. Its rich blossoms and large, fragrant flowers are so breathtaking. The unique shape of the branches and the large buds are poetic and will add to the look of many Ikebana arrangements. The satiny, fragrant pink blossoms of tulip magnolia are a lovely treat in the depths of winter. Both in bud stage and in bloom, these flowering branches add natural beauty and sculptural form to any décor. In this arrangement, I combined several branches of tulip magnolia to create this composition. When

it's hard to find a single fine, ideal branch, you can assemble it in the vase by yourself!

When creating an arrangement with a single floral material, combine them asymmetrically with different lengths and angles. It may look simple, but it uses a variety of techniques, so your arrangement will never be dull.

The choice of vase should also be carefully considered. I love using this vase, because the austere texture makes any simple arrangement look stunning. Also, its shoulder parts make it easy to hold the heavy materials, and its big volume balances out the large branches.

Lilac, Snowball Viburnum, and Pittosporum
Vase: Susumu Zaima

Lilac flowers are pleasantly fragrant and add a beautiful lavender color to arrangements. Snowball viburnum is prized for its round clusters of white flowers that resemble snowballs. Both flowers' clusters make a showy display and are exquisite in Ikebana arrangements. But both branches need proper care before and after you create your arrangements to help them stay hydrated. Split the cut end of the branches lengthwise and peel off the last few inches of the bark with scissors and then immediately put them in water with plant food added.

As you now know, most Ikebana arrangements are based on asymmetrical balance. This arrangement is no exception. The leaves of pittosporum have been added to create a connection between the lilac and snowball viburnum. Create this arrangement with a bold horizontal line on one side only. If this composition had some materials on both sides, it would lose visual strength. Note that this vase has shoulders, so it is much easier to fix floral materials to successfully create an arrangement that's in horizontal style.

Flowering Quince and Freesia
Vase: Antique White Porcelain Vase

This large arrangement features an intricate design lending an eye-catching presence, using brilliant red flowering quince with yellow freesias as a fresh accent. One branch is positioned on the right side of the vase, and three small branches and freesias are added on the left side, creating a splendid scene.

The large branch on the right side works as a fixture for the other materials that are placed on the left side. As you can see, the composition of this arrangement is simple, regardless of how it looks. When arranging a branch or flower lower than the rim of the vase, bend it at the desired angle.

Olive tree branches are my favorite. They are from ancient times and cared for with respect for the surrounding environment. The olive branch was often a symbol of abundance, glory, and peace. They are vibrant under the bright sunshine in Santa Monica and their relaxed and healthy organic look is just so perfect for the vibe of this city. Olive branches give Ikebana arrangements that same vibe.

Olive trees have lovely silver leaves, which complement many other flowers. I am lucky enough to have large olive trees in my community, so I can prune fresh branches whenever I need them. They're easy to care for and they look good, so I have a small olive tree at my front door as well.

Olive Tree Branches Strelitzia and Pumpkin Tree

Place the olive branches first, and then cross them to support each other. It will make it easier for other floral materials to be added to stay in place. Next, add pumpkin trees in the middle of the arrangement. Then insert two stems of strelitzia in different lengths and directions.

The cluttered look of the olive branches is settled together by placing the other materials in the middle. The orange color is the "mass" and green color is the "lines."

It's important to create depth as well as height and width.

Olive Tree and Butterfly Ranunculus

This is a very plain Ikebana arrangement; branches and flowers are simply placed straight into a kenzan. Rather than sticking to techniques and rules, I prioritize bringing out the beauty of the floral materials. I love this bohemian finish of the olive branches and butterfly ranunculus.

Dried Branches as a Decorative Fixture

The decorative fixture of dried branches not only looks beautiful, but also functions perfectly as a fixture. Thus, this technique is often used in ikebana.

Dried branches can be used over and over again in various arrangements, and depending on the coordination or the other components, they can give a completely different impression.

Dried Grapewood Branches

Sandblasted grapewood branches are very common driftwoods sold in floral supply stores, so if you don't live near the beach or a forest where you can collect your own, don't worry!

In Ikebana, we often use large driftwoods with flowers and foliage, especially at Ikebana exhibitions, when I need to create a larger arrangement. These abstract and sculptural shapes help me to arrange a dynamic, artistic movement effortlessly.

Open your mind to what will look good in an arrangement. It is not always about the perfect-looking bloom; wild grasses and unusual shapes shake up an arrangement and set it apart from the norm.

Dried Grapewood Branches, Kale, Tulip and Camellia Leaf
Vase: Concrete Pot

The dried grapewood branches rise to the upper right and give a sense of impact and dynamism. The flowers and leaves entwined in the branches give a sense of vitality. They are not all facing the front but can be angled sideways or backward to create a sense of natural movement and depth.

The branches act as a fixture, making it very easy to secure the flowers and foliage. When finished, add enough water.

Assemble the driftwood in any combination you like. This is the fun part and because any combination can look amazingly stunning. The branch lines can protrude from the vase and continue onto the table, you are free to use any combination.

Once you have settled on the shape you desire, secure the branches with wire.

For larger arrangements like this one, if the stems do not reach the water in the vase, you can use floral water tubes.

Ikebana Edibles

Creating Ikebana arrangements using fruits and vegetables may be a totally unexpected idea for you.

In the Sogetsu textbook that I use in my Ikebana class, lessons on fruit and vegetable arrangements are a part of the curriculum. These arrangements are called Morimono, which allows for any part of the plant to be used to create Ikebana.

To be honest, I wasn't particularly enthusiastic about creating arrangements with fruits and vegetables when I first became interested in Ikebana until I saw some beautifully dramatic vegetables at a local farmer's market in Santa Monica. I found colorful cauliflowers in purple and orange, green onions with their roots still attached, Swiss chard with their glossy green leaves and bright red stems, butter lettuce layered like the petals of a flower, Romanesco broccoli with its natural fractal form, and many fresh herbs. I have been captivated by their lovely looks ever since. Under the bright sun, the rainbow of fruits and vegetables shine.

Whether you like the taste or not, there are many beautifully formed produce items. When I go to the farmer's market, I am not only looking for groceries, but also for materials for my Ikebana! Earth's bounty provides so many great options for arrangements.

Here is an opportunity for you to create unique arrangements using fruits and vegetables as the main materials. It is best not to stray too far from the fruits' and vegetables' natural forms, so don't alter their structure when arranging them. When you create art from fruits and vegetables, it is another way to reveal their true beauty and it allows you to see what you are familiar with in a new way. Your arrangement doesn't have to contain only fruits and vegetables, though. You can use other elements as well, but using fruit or vegetables as the focal point is eye-catching and interesting because it is an unexpected way to add unique textures to Ikebana.

Create Your Work Space

- Either select a vase for your arrangement or, if you have a piece of fruit or vegetable that can be hollowed out to create a vessel, that can also be used. Some fruits or vegetables that can be made into interesting vessels are gourds, pumpkins, eggplant, or Japanese watermelon.

- Place your kenzan at the bottom of the vase, bowl, or hollowed produce if you are using a shallow vessel.

- Place your scissors where they are easily available.

- Place the fruits or vegetables you have chosen to include in the arrangement on the work service.

- Observe each carefully to find the most beautiful angle.

- Take a few moments to visualize how they can be combined into an arrangement that will be visually interesting.

Fig Branch and Cosmos
Vase: Astier de Villatte

In this arrangement, the figs are arranged like ornaments with the leaves removed from the branches so that the fruit can be clearly seen.

Cosmos leaves with narrow lobes and hairy margins are placed to add a gentle but dramatic and airy feel.

The composition is similar to the basic style, which has three lines creating three-dimensional space. The weight of the arrangement is on the left side, and so that the right side has negative space.

"Direct fixing" is applied in this arrangement. Lean the tall line of the cosmos stem slightly backward to create an open space.

Combining figs with leaves that are completely different from their original leaves reveals their charm.

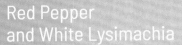

Red Pepper
and White Lysimachia
Vase: Susumu Zaima

These peppers are sure to spice up any
arrangement. The vivid red color of the
peppers is more powerful than the delicate
red flowers, giving the arrangement extra
energy and strength. The red peppers
and the green leaves create a good
rhythm, and the small white flowers of
lysimachia provide a graceful accent to the
overall arrangement.

I love to decorate my house with
their vibrant red to cheer and
encourage my family. And the pepper
arrangement is uncommon, so when people
see it, they are always surprised

Purple and Yellow Broccoli, Romanesco Broccoli, and Broccoli Flower
Vase: Hasami Porcelain

I absolutely adore this combination of various broccoli and broccoli flowers arranged together like a broccoli patch. The bright contrast of purple, green, and yellow broccoli creates a joyful harvest arrangement. The lime-green Romanesco broccoli in the middle of the vase has a stunning pattern of geometric curves with its fractal head and crown-like florets, which is so eye-catching

Swiss Chard and Safflower
Vase: Susumu Zaima

Swiss chard is a leafy vegetable that is related to beets. It has crunchy stems that are commonly red, though can also be white or yellow.
The leaves are shiny and dark green, with a grooved, bumpy texture, which is so mobile and expressive for Ikebana arrangements.

In this arrangement, I rolled up the leaves and randomly placed them in the vase. When the swiss chard leaves are rolled, they look more abundant and very artistic.

Insert the detached red stems of the swiss chard and safflowers between the leaves as bright accents.

Just as swiss chard can be made into a quick and easy dish with minimal prep, an Ikebana arrangement with it can also be made into quick and easy artwork.

Lemon Branch
and Dark Opal Basil
Vase: Susumu Zaima

Carefully identify the front and back of the lemon branch, as the front side has to face forward. Trim the excess leaves of the lemon branch and position it so that the beautiful curve points upward. In expressing the brilliance or vitality of floral materials, it is important to arrange them at an upward angle, in a way that makes use of the vibrant energy.

Insert the dark opal basils in a flowing motion to the left side of the vase. The overall impression of this arrangement is that the right line of the lemon branch is connected to the left line of the dark opal basils, forming a large undulating curve.

"Direct fixing" is applied here. As shown in the picture, the branch is fixed at two points in the vase: the inner wall and the rim.

Even just cutting the branches, I could smell the nice citrus scent—it was like aromatherapy with lemon!

I chose this branch because of this unique shape; a lemon is pinched between the branches. I love to arrange something unusual to surprise viewers. The more imperfect something is, the more interesting and meaningful it is.

The fruits and vegetables presented in this book were cooked and eaten after the arrangements were finished. After this particular arrangement, the lemons were made into lemon water and salad dressing.

Back to Nature

Due to my mother's influence, I've been exposed to antiques and beautiful rustic objects since I was a girl. She displayed them tastefully in our house. She often took my sister and me to museums that included Japanese antiques. So I naturally developed a love for beautiful and rustic things. Like my mother, I have been collecting those objects little by little.

I enjoy using some of the austere vases I have collected to create Ikebana in a rustic and natural style. The way you arrange flowers is important, but so is the vase. Your vase becomes a part of your work and will affect how the arrangement looks.

I like to use baskets and Japanese vases, but old items, such as antique vases, and even broken and imperfect knickknacks, can be repurposed and used in Ikebana arrangements. In fact, I often get inspiration from vases. I enjoy going to antique stores and flea markets to look for interesting pieces.

When arranging rustic and natural style Ikebana, simple materials and loose, airy movements are the point. Make the viewer feel a gentle breeze, with a slightly unruly look. You need to pay extra attention to alignment and organize all the feet of the stems to create a harmonious and cohesive look, otherwise the arrangement might look messy and chaotic.

It's time to create a rustic-yet-sophisticated arrangement using Ikebana. The idea is for it to be different from a Western-style arrangement while keeping a casual, farmstead style.

This is a great project if you have a garden you can take a mix of cuttings from to personalize your design. For this arrangement, it's best to use garden-grown flowers or wildflowers. I sometimes utilize olive branches, small flowers, and delicate foliage from the community where I live. Dried flowers work well in this style as well.

Ikebana doesn't have to be something that only looks good in Japanese-style interiors, nor does it have to be wabi-sabi chic. In any country, any region, with any flower or vessel, you can create a wonderful Ikebana. Each person will have their own style. The possibilities are endless, so let's find your original style.

Create Your Work Space

- Select a vessel for your arrangement and fill it with water.
- Place your kenzan at the bottom of the vase or bowl if you are using a shallow vessel.
- Place your scissors where they are easily available.
- Gather a variety of flowers in different colors, sizes, and textures, and place them in a vase of water to keep them hydrated until it is time for the stems to be cut and placed.
- Observe each element carefully to find the most beautiful angle of flower, leaf, or branch.

Crabapple, Grevillea, and Alstroemeria
Vase: Bizen Ware Vase

Known for their fragrant springtime blooms and jewel-like fruits, crabapple trees make beautiful additions to the landscape.

I created this crabapple arrangement in autumn, so the changing color of the leaves evokes the atmosphere of the season. The branches are softly falling downward, so their lines can be used to create a rustic and natural arrangement. Also, for the theme of this chapter, I picked a Bizen ware vase, which has an earthen-like, reddish-brown color and an organic feeling.

As you have learned already, branches are often used as the framework of an Ikebana arrangement, so start by placing the crabapple branches first. Before you start making your arrangement, observe the branches one by one in your hands and find their most pleasing sides.

The first branch is placed in the vase with "direct fixing" and will also work as a fixture inside the vase so that the next branches will be easily fixed in place as well.

Carefully add in more branches one by one until you feel that you have achieved the aesthetic you want. Arrange branches in such a way that they eventually cross inside the vase and support each other.

In this arrangement, some twigs were left on the branches to keep a rustic look.

Insert the branches on the back side as well as the front side to balance the overall arrangement. The more branches you add, the easier it will be to stabilize the material.

Place three stems of grevillea in the vase at different angles and lengths to add volume. The color of grevillea and crabapple branches are the same tone, so this arrangement has a quiet but vibrant harmony.

To finish up, tuck in one or two stems of alstroemeria. Alstroemeria has multiple flowers on a single stem, but you can take those flowers apart and arrange them separately if you would like.

After a while, the branches and flowers wither, but you can rearrange the remaining healthy materials.

From the previous arrangement, alstroemeria was removed; instead, two stems of rudbeckia flower and ruscus leaves were added. We can still enjoy the minimal beauty of Ikebana even with a small amount of floral material.

This is a rearrangement of crabapple branches in an upright style. Examine the angle of each branch carefully to bring about a beautiful balance.

Crabapple

Vase: Susumu Zaima

With their tiny red fruits popping up on the branches, crabapples are something of a botanical lollipop. In this arrangement, the autumn branches with tiny apples are positioned horizontally, as if the branches were draped over a table and vase. I chose a rustic vase and decided to create the arrangement to look like it was part of nature, without adding any other material.

Using a single type of branch creates a quiet movement. The wall of the vase hides the kenzan, so you don't have to worry about hiding it.

Note that the branch crossing over the vase and the one at the back are placed directly on the table, rather than in the vase. Only a small branch is placed in the vase.

In Ikebana, branches are often arranged outside the vase. This technique allows you to create more flexible and expressive designs.

When arranging branches, I observe each branch very carefully and select my favorite shapes. If necessary, disassemble, rebuild, bend, and trim excess twigs and leaves to create more ideal forms.

Mock Orange, Lavender, Lisianthus and Bupleurum
Vase: Bamboo Basket by Kohchosai Kosuga

Using a basket rather than a vase to hold the botanicals in place is a perfect way to create rustic looking arrangements. I picked a bamboo basket that was hand-woven and dyed in black with Japanese lacquer in Kyoto, Japan.

Because this is a small basket, I used small, delicate flowers for a good sense of proportion and harmony.

A small glass vase inside the basket is used to hold the flowers in place and keep them hydrated.

Alstroemeria, Snowberry, Baby's Breath, and Maple Leaf

This arrangement is made with very few floral materials, but they are placed only on the left side of the basket to create a sense of drama. A maple leaf is added as a gentle accent.

California Pepper Tree and Scabiosa

Vase: Susumu Zaima

Note: when you display a square or rectangular vase, place it diagonally. If the vase is placed parallel to the viewers, the balance between the arrangement and vase will be diminished.

To begin, place a kenzan in the corner of the vase, not in the center. Next, arrange the drooping branches of the California pepper tree as they would be found in nature. Extra leaves should be trimmed to show the beautiful curves of branches. If there are branches tangled together, untangle them to give each one space.

Scabiosa flowers should be placed like flowers resting in the shade of a tree, to make this arrangement have a peaceful and poetic aesthetic.

The California pepper tree looks very attractive from both the side and the top view, so it is great to display on a lower table.

Cosmos, Explosion Grass, and Filipendula

Vase: Bamboo Basket by Kohchosai Kosuga

Flowers suggest the season or occasion, creating a mood both of their own and in harmony with their container. A rough, homey container is chosen for this lacy arrangement as if cosmos flowers are blooming in a meadow. The natural color of a Shikainami bamboo basket enhances this rustic look.

For this arrangement, create a wild profusion of flowers that looks as if they have naturally grown out of the basket. To emphasize the motion of the arrangement, keep the overall form open and airy. The explosion grass and filipendula are added to enhance the sense of movement. The grass is also put out through the gaps in the basket to create a more natural feeling.

Don't adjust too much; let the floral materials guide you.

Cosmos flowers and other floral materials are arranged at various heights and angles in all directions to emphasize the natural and rustic style.

A small glass vase with a kenzan is placed in the basket to hold the floral material and to hold water. If the vase that can be seen through the gaps of the basket, it becomes a part of the scenery.

Clematis, Scabiosa, Foxtail Millet, and Explosion Grass
Vase: Bamboo Basket by Kohchosai Kosuga

Clematis, with its delicate and flexible vine and lovely bell-like flowers, is perfect for rustic Ikebana. The flowers are beautiful both facing up and down.

I created this arrangement with clematis vines crawling inside a basket and coming out through the gaps in the weave. To make it the focus, the other floral materials are arranged low. Clematis leaves are vividly arranged in various directions to create a more natural look. Most of the materials are placed on the right side of the basket to add drama to the arrangement.

Two different sized glass vases are placed inside the basket to hold the floral materials. It's useful to have a variety of glass vases, but if you don't have any on hand, you can use empty jars or bottles as well.

Pampas Grass, Foxtail Millet, Love-in-a-Mist, and Explosion Grass

Vase: Pottery Bowl

Even when creating rustic-style arrangements, it is important to have intentional harmony. This arrangement is a simple composition with rustic floral materials and a vase.

Place a kenzan in the corner of the vase, and then insert the materials at different lengths and in different directions. If possible, arrange the bottom of the stems close together so that the overall arrangement looks organized.

To complete the arrangement, add the tassel-like foxtail millet that resembles the vase color as a subtle accent.

Nandina, White Lysimachia, and Veronica
Vase: Recycled Glass Vase

When my mom used to welcome guests into our house, she always had an arrangement of beautiful greenery in a large urn in the hallway near the gate to the front door. Since I started learning Ikebana, I often visualize my mother arranging flowers as she did when I was a child. While making this arrangement, I was reminded of those old memories.

I placed nandina branches on the right side of the case, and white lysimachia and veronica on the left side. I wanted to create a natural look, so I kept the composition simple.

Examine the nandina branches carefully to find the beautiful and suitable ones for your arrangement. If necessary, trim, bend, or shape the branches to your liking.

Glossary of Ikebana Terms

Chabana: translated as "tea flowers"; refers specifically to the flower display in the tea room.

Chadō: the tea ceremony.

Color: You can determine whether colors are complementary or contrasting by consulting a color wheel. The closer colors are to each other on the wheel, the more they are in harmony. If they are across from each other on a color wheel, they are contrasting. You can also create Ikebana using only one color.

Flow: movement while placing the flowers to create the arrangement.

Freestyle: This technique is divided into two types: arrangements that are naturalistic, and those that are abstract and emphasize design rather than nature.

Floral Frog: A kenzan.

Ikenobo Senkei: the Buddhist priest of Kyoto Rokkakudo; appeared in historical records in 1462 as "master of flower arranging," so he is considered the one who established the philosophy and technique of Ikebana.

Kenzan: an object composed of a heavy lead plate covered in sharp pins. Its pins pierce through the bases of the stems to hold them in the desired position.

Line: the sculptural element created by the branches and stems, as well as with the space around them. The branches and stems used in Ikebana are as important as the flowers because they create visual structure and rhythm. The idea is to be minimalist and asymmetrical while creating balanced harmony.

Mass: the density of materials within the arrangement—how close together they are and how much space is between the blooms and stems, which creates an emphasis and sometimes a focal point within the arrangement.

Moribana: translated as "piled up flowers"; a style of Ikebana which is using a kenzan in a shallow vase.

Nageire: translated as "throw-in"; a style of vertically or horizontally orientated arrangement that often uses a narrow-mouthed, tall vase without a kenzan.

Rikka: derived from Tatebana and, like Tatebana, is translated as "standing flowers." This opulent form became popular among wealthy townspeople.

Shoka or Seika: translated as "fresh flowers"; classical in appearance but asymmetrical in structure.

Tatebana: translated as "standing flowers"; became a popular form of flower arranging among the samurai class and aristocracy.

About the Author

Naoko Zaimais teaches classes in creating Ikebana arrangements and sells her arrangements through local stores. She is very affirming and believes that all Ikebana is precious, beautiful, and loveable—because it has been created using a sense of feeling and reflects a person's spirit and state of mind. She has also recently started a minimalist jewelry business called *The Sheek*. She is from Japan, but now lives in Santa Monica, California.

Instagram: @zaimanaoko

yellow pear 🍐 press

Yellow Pear Press, established in 2015, publishes inspiring, charming, clever, distinctive, playful, imaginative, beautifully designed lifestyle books, cookbooks, literary fiction, notecards, and journals with a certain *joie de vivre* in both content and style. Yellow Pear Press books have been honored by the Independent Publisher Book (IPPY) Awards, National Indie Excellence Awards, Independent Press Awards, and International Book Awards. Reviews of our titles have appeared in Kirkus Reviews, Foreword Reviews, Booklist, Midwest Book Review, San Francisco Chronicle, and New York Journal of Books, among others. Yellow Pear Press joined forces with Mango Publishing in 2020, with the vision to continue publishing clever and innovative books. The fact that they're both named after fruit is a total coincidence.

We love hearing from our readers, so please stay in touch with us and follow us at:

Facebook: Mango Publishing
Instagram: @MangoPublishing
LinkedIn: Mango Publishing
Pinterest: Mango Publishing

Newsletter: mangopublishinggroup.com/newsletter